THE BEST OF

Books and Company

THE BEST OF

Books and Company

ABOUT BOOKS FOR
THOSE WHO DELIGHT IN THEM

EDITED BY

Susan Hill

LONG BARN BOOKS

PUBLISHED BY
LONG BARN BOOKS

Ebrington Gloucestershire GL55 6NW

First published 2010

Set in Centaur

Printed and bound by J F Print Ltd, Sparkford, Somerset

ISBN: 978-1-902421-42-1

Contents

FOREWORD

I cannot trace the source of the saying 'all writers have to start a small magazine once in their lives' and it is perhaps less true than it was. The expected readership for one was never large but these days it would be even smaller.

Having founded, compiled, edited and published *Books and Company* for four years I can safely say 'never again,' for many reasons though principally the usual one – lack of time. All the same, it was very enjoyable, I learned a lot and a lot of people liked it. Second hand copies, and especially complete runs of the magazine are much sought–after and I am often asked if I will begin all over again. No, I will not. The main reason for its abrupt cessation, however, was not any change of heart on my part but a fire in the barn where my office was, which destroyed the entire working database and mailing list. The thought of trying to reconstitute those made me lose the will to live and so the demise of *Books and Company* came about by fate rather than by any decision of mine.

From the beginning though, I had intended to compile this anthology. So many fine writers contributed to the magazine that it would be a disgrace not to give their pieces a wider audience and a more permanent home. I am grateful to everyone who so willingly and generously wrote for *Books and Company* and to all the subscribers, most of whom remained loyal over its lifetime.

SUSAN HILL

A roof of one's own

Jeanette Winterson

I used to live in Water Street. In a two-up two-down, as they used to be called, to distinguish those houses from the inferior back-to-backs which had only one room on each floor and no yard.

Water Street was cobbled then and had been, once, the line of a watercourse that ran from the Heights down a steep hill and into the valley that became a town.

Watercourse no longer, the street was a conduit for the daily life of mothers and children flowing from house to house.

In the summertime it was the custom for the doors onto the street to be left open, the entrance shielded by strips of coloured plastic threaded on a rod and hung on a pair of cup hooks. These bright waterfalls signalled welcome and gossip. The form was to pause outside and shout 'Are you in?' and the reply would come back, 'I am.'

For the children on either side of the waterfall this was the moment of escape. We escaped into each other, into our own inventiveness. For me it became an escape into a secret of my own; a stone-age library.

One day, like the tadpoles we were, we darted away from Water Street and squirmed under the gates of the derelict, once glorious, Accrington Stanley football ground.

While my friends were frightening themselves in the ghostly changing rooms, I found a stockpile of short square roofing slates. I picked up a stone and started drawing on one; cats, dogs, flowers, my mummy with and without her bosom – the usual things.. Then I started writing on them; bits of hymns, poems from memory, and I realized that I could make for myself all the books I could not buy.

This is how it was done.

First of all I borrowed a book from the library. This would be examined by my mother for harmful influences and then handed back to me for one week only.

Since I was not allowed to take library books out of the house my next move was to memorise as much of the text as I could. Then as soon as somebody appeared outside the waterfall curtain, I fled the house and copied down my lines on the slates. I had no chalk so my writing had to be done with a stone.

The only way to memorize a book is to say it out loud to yourself and I did this, gabbling away as children do, my real purpose concealed because nobody ever listens to what a child has to say.

'Jeanette, come and eat this potato pie.'

'But the hour came at last that ended Mr Earnshaw's troubles upon earth.'

'Do you want pickled onion with it?'

'He died quietly in his chair one October evening, seated by the fireside.'

'Or you can have tomato sauce.'

'A high wind blustered round the house and roared in the chimney; it sounded wild and stormy yet it was not cold.'

'It was hot when it came out of the oven.'

Eighteenth and nineteenth century classics are long. My slates were short. I could not copy word for word and more and more I sought to transpose what seemed to me essential and to add the connectives myself in shorthand devised for the purpose.

Pirate I was, sailing on the forward momentum of someone else's prose and then tacking on a spit's length of my own.

I know this is an author's nightmare and that my stone-age library breached every nicety of copyright and scholarship. At least I was not boiling down *Reader's Digest*-style abridgements. It was not the story I wanted, I wanted those moments of intensity that change a narrative into a poem. I wanted to feel its heartbeat against my own.

What worlds could I not inhabit if those worlds existed in books? I never thought of myself as a poor chid from Lancashire, I thought of myself as Aladdin, Hotspur, Lancelot, Heathcliff. Not gender, not time, not circumstance seemed any barrier to me. The book was a door. Open it. Pass freely.

Barriers there were, largely my mother, who always placed her ample frame in front of my small doorways. A pamphleteer by temperament, she knew that sedition and controversy are fired by printed matter. She knew the power of books and so she avoided them, countering their influence with exhortations of her own, single sheets pasted about the house. It was quite normal for me to find a little sermon in my packed lunch or a few Bible verses, with commentary, stuffed into my hockey boots. Fed words and shod with them, words became clues. I hunted them down, knowing they would lead me to something valuable, something beyond myself and whether that something was inside or outside, in action or imagination, hardly mattered.

My mother suspected me of harbouring print. She searched thoroughly but found nothing. Library books that were vetted and returned never worried her, it was close association that she feared – that a book might fall into my hands and remain there. It never occurred to her that I fell into books, that I put myself for safe-keeping inside them. When I copied them out later it was myself I was freeing.

Freedom, not escapism. Time with a book is not time away from the real world. A book is its own world, unique, entire. A place we choose to visit, and although we cannot stay there, something of the book stays with us, perhaps vividly, perhaps out of conscious memory altogether, until years later we find it again, forgotten in a pocket, like a shell from a beach.

Freedom, the chance to enlarge mind and spirit beyond the confines of the everyday. The everyday will crush us if it can. Art acts as a canopy against the downward pressure of mass. Like titanium, it is strong, light and resistant to corrosion.

Many a time I have taken shelter under a book. I do not think of art as consolation, rather I think of it as a roof over my head. There is good reason for this when your books are made of slates, but there are other reasons too...

Since I left home as a teenager I have had nineteen different homes. A considerable number I think for someone who is thirty-eight and not a Foreign Correspondent. I like where I live whenever I live in it but I never expect to be able to stay. For the first ten years or so it was love and money; either I couldn't afford to stay or I romantically evicted myself. More lately I am in pursuit of something even more elusive than the perfect redhead but the outcome is the same. I don't stay anywhere for long.

Always leaving, what can I take with me?

Books. Books written and not. Other people's and my own. Books are home. They don't make a home, they are one.

If my mother had had her way I would have lived out my life in her own grey tower planted round with thorns. My mother was an unhappy woman, difficult and intense. I was a happy child, also difficult and intense. The battle between us, really that of happiness and unhappiness, was somehow bound up in the battle of the books. Her charge against reading –'You never know what's in a book until it's too late' – taught me how powerful books are. When you side with a book, its strength becomes your strength. My mother did not want me to become strong on books. She knew she would lose me if I did. I wanted books because I did not want to be her Rapunzel. There was no prince to rescue me. (I had guessed by now that I would be doing most of the prince-work myself) but I was determined to be carried away by a story.

What do stories tell us? That this life is a journey through a dark wood. That the soul is always in peril. That those who love should never count the cost. That duty and passion tear the heart in half. That beauty is as good a reason as any. That understanding is all. That miracles happen. That there are heroes. That even a hero like Siegfried, who can row against the current of the Rhine, is destroyed by his own vanity and forgetfulness. That wisdom is pain but pain is not wisdom. That the buried treasure is really there. That few things are worth the burden of possession. That no one can steal what no one can possess. That there is always a second chance. That there is love.

And these things need to be said in every different way for every different generation, again and again. Underneath time is perpetuity. The connectedness of history and DNA. What we make and what we are, splinted together and anatomized for us in art.

The clean slate that is the child is also the coded carrier of the universe. We are what is written and what is read.

We are the living book.

Jeanette Winterson is the author of Oranges Are Not The Only Fruit, The Passion, Sexing the Cherry *and many other novels, collections of essays and adaptations. She has been awarded the Whitbread Prize, the Prix d'argent, the John Llewellyn Rhys Prize, a BAFTA, the Commonwealth Writers prize and an OBE.*

Why do we read?

Alain de Boton

People who love books are often assumed to belong to a single category. A pink letter comes through the letterbox. It is from a dating agency, which, in a well-meaning (unsolicited) attempt to find me a partner requests that I fill out a questionnaire. I am asked whether, on weekend, I prefer playing sport, gardening, cooking, watching television or reading. A premise that two people who love books will stand a good chance of liking one another.

However charming the idea, it fails to pick up on the extraordinary diversity of reasons why people read, and hence on the dangers of conflict arising between two people who are otherwise both attached to spending weekends quietly between hard covers.

One might make a most basic distinction between motives for reading – on the one hand, reading to escape oneself, on the other, reading to find oneself. The former is particularly well addressed at station news-stands. Marooned in anxious or tedious circumstances, there is pleasure in buying a paperback before a journey, in involving ourselves in a story of ten generations in a Southern American town or in the quest to find the murderer of a CIA agent decapitated in an internet café. Once we've boarded a carriage, we can abstract ourselves from current surroundings and enter a more agreeable, or at least agreeably different world, breaking out occasionally to take in the passing scenery, while holding open our badly printed volume at the point where a detective has let off a gun, or a farmhand has kissed the heroine – until our destination is announced, the brakes let out their reluctant squeals, and we emerge once more into reality, symbolized by the station and its group of loitering slate-grey pigeons pecking shiftily at abandoned confectionery.

Then there is the pleasure of reading to find oneself. There are authors who seem to express our very own thoughts, but with a clarity and psychological accuracy we could not match. They know us better than we know ourselves. What was shy and confused within us, is unapologetically and cogently phrased in them, our pencil-lines in the margins of these books indicating where we have found a piece of ourselves, a sentence or two built of the very substance of which our own minds are made, a congruence all the more striking if the work was written by someone in an age of top-hats or togas. We feel grateful to these strangers for reminding us of who we are.

There may be an analogy to be made between love and reading. A few years ago, I was browsing in a bookshop when my eye was caught by a quote on the cover of a paperback: 'To be psychologically alive means either being in love, or in psychoanalysis, or in the spell of literature'. The book was called *Tales of Love*, it was written by the French psychoanalyst Julia Kristeva, and I was tempted enough to buy it. Unfortunately, the analyst let me down badly, for in over three hundred pages, she did nothing to elaborate on the fascinating sentence that her publisher had so cunningly placed on the back cover.

Still, the thought seemed valuable and stayed with me, of

an important connection between love and reading, of a comparable pleasure offered by both. A feeling of connection may be at the root of it. There are books which speak to us, no less intensely – but more reliably – than our lovers. They prevent the morose suspicion that we do not fully belong to the human species, that we lie beyond comprehension. Our embarrassments, our sulks, our feelings of guilt, these phenomena may be conveyed on a page in a way that affords us a sense of self-recognition. The author has located words to depict a situation we thought ourselves alone in feeling, and for a few moments, we are like two lovers on an early dinner date thrilled to discover how much they share (and so unable to do more than graze at the food in front of them), we may place the book down for a second and stare at its spine with a wry smile, as if to say, 'How lucky I ran into you.'

Marcel Proust seems to have been saying something similar when, towards the end of his long book, he wrote, 'In reality, each reader reads only what is already within himself. The book is only a sort of optical instrument which the writer offers to the reader to enable the latter to discover what he would not have found but for the aid of the book.' The value of great books isn't limited to the depiction of emotions and people akin to those in our own life, it stretches to an ability to describe these far better than we would have been able, to put a finger on perceptions that we both recognize as our own, but could not have formulated on our own.

If we are able to relate our experiences to those described in great books written long ago, it is perhaps because there are fewer human types than there are people. Arthur Schopenhauer suggested that every great writer was able to bring out the universal dimension of local phenomena. Hamlet is one character in a play set at the Danish court, and yet there were, Schopenhauer pointed out, several Hamlets living unhappily and moodily in Frankfurt in the middle of the nineteenth century, as there must be Hamlets in London at the end of the twentieth. The genius of Shakespeare was to thread together disparate characteristics and so define a permanent human possibility. Mario Vargas Llosa remarked that, growing up in Peru, he had known many Emma Bovarys.

It may explain why literature can offer relief when love has failed. When I first read Goethe's *Sorrows of Young Werther*, I was at university, twenty one and, of course, Werther. Lotte was Claire (she lived along the corridor, studied biology and had shoulder-length chestnut hair in a centre parting) and Albert was played by Robin, an economist who she'd been seeing for three years – testimony, if one needs it, of the ability of novels to mould themselves around, and illuminate, our own lives. Recognizing ourselves in works of art enables us to adopt a consoling perspective on our own troubles, for we can learn to view events from the universal standpoint which writers have themselves taken in order to create their work. Schopenhauer, who had met and much admired Goethe, believed that after reading a great love story like Werther, a man who had suffered a romantic rejection would see that he had experienced a universal kind of pain, not a personal, isolated curse. 'Such a reader will look less at his own individual lot than at the lot of mankind as a whole, and accordingly will conduct himself as a knower rather than as a sufferer.'

The idea that we are not alone in the world can be cosy. Nevertheless, we may still be attached to feeling unique, and this is not something literature suggests we in fact are. Take the following: 'Some people would never have fallen in love if they had not heard there was such a thing.' I recall reading this maxim from La Rochefoucauld on a flight between London and Edinburgh. 'That's my idea,' was my immediate response, and I stared out of the window at the cottony Midlands in some confusion. 'He's stolen my thought.' But it seemed unlikely, given that he was born in the spring of 1613 and I in 1969, so more generously, I reflected, 'Maybe I've stolen it from him' – equally impossible, given that I had until then never laid eyes on the Maxims.

It suggested an answer at once humbling and ennobling: that both La Rochefoucauld and I had lived in the same world, and could hence at times be expected to think roughly the same thoughts, even though he was a genius and I am not (La Rochefoucauld would immediately have picked up on the self-pity in this last comment, and could well have squashed it with a withering: 'There are few people more convinced of their own genius than those who complain of how stupid they are.') It is an idea that threatens our sense of identity, which is based so much on difference. What if exposure to literature reveals too much of what we have in common with others? What can we say – and write – if all our most private experiences turn out to be the well-trodden thinking grounds of other writers?

Part of learning to read – and by implication to write – is accepting that our personalities are not as water-tight as we like to imagine, that many things which we think of as private are in fact not very personal. This is not to say they are impersonal, a word invoking the service in fast-food restaurants, rather that they are common to all human beings. The price of discovering that we are not so isolated is a recognition that we are also far from unique.

Alain de Botton is the author of three novels and the bestselling How Proust Can Change Your Life, *as well as other works of essayistic non-fiction which have been described as a 'philosophy of everyday life'. He is the founder of The School of Life, in London.*

How I discovered books

Roger Scruton

Although my father was a teacher, books did not play a large part in our home. Those that could be found in the house were of a useful or improving kind – encyclopaedias, the Bible, Palgrave's *Golden Treasury*, some gardening books, the Penguin *Odyssey* and memoirs of the Second World War. My mother dabbled a little in exotic religions, which meant that pamphlets by Indian gurus would from time to time occupy the front room table. But neither she nor my father had any conception of the Book, as a hidden door in the scheme of things which opens into another world.

My first inkling of this experience came from Bunyan. The year was 1957. I was thirteen, a day-boy at our next-door grammar school, where I learned to distinguish books in two kinds- on the syllabus and off it. *Pilgrim's Progress* must surely have been off the syllabus- nothing else can account for the astonishment with which I turned its pages. I was convalescing from 'flu, sitting in the garden on a fine spring day. A few yards to my left was our house – a plain, whitewashed Edwardian box, part of a ribbon development that stretched along the main road from High Wycombe half way to Amersham. To the right stood the neo-Georgian Grammar School with its frontage of lawn, opposite was the ugly new housing estate which spoiled our view. I sat in a nondescript corner of post-war England; nothing could conceivably happen in such surroundings except the things that happen anywhere- a bus passing, a dog barking, football on the wireless, shepherd's pie for tea.

And then, suddenly, I was in a visionary landscape where even the most ordinary things come dressed in astonishment. In Bunyan's world words are not barriers or defences, as they are in suburban England but messages sent to the heart. They jump into you from the page, as though in answer to a summons. This, surely, is the sign of a great writer; that he speaks to you in your voice by making his voice your own.

I did not put the book down until I had finished. And for months afterwards I strode through our suburb side-by-side with Pilgrim, my inner eye fixed on the City of Light.

Two years later, when I was studying A level science, my parents decided to move. They had found a house in Marlow, smaller, quieter and quainter than Amersham Road. The owners – a retired couple called Deas who were emigrating to Canada – drove over to discuss the deal. I was left sitting in the same spot in our garden drinking tea with their son.

Since Bunyan, few books off the syllabus had passed through my hands. Nevertheless, I had heard rumours of the artistic temperament, and something about Ivor Deas made me suspect that he suffered from this obscure but distinguished ailment. He was a bachelor of some forty years, still living with his parents. His face was pale and thin, with grey eyes that seemed to fade away when you looked at them. His alabaster hands with their long white fingers, his quiet voice; his spare and careful words, his trousers rubbed shiny at the knees and the Adam's apple shifting up and down, like a ping-pong ball in a fountain – all of these seemed totally out of place in our suburb, and conferred on him an air of suffering fragility that must surely have some literary cause. He sat in silence, waiting for me to speak. I asked him his occupation. He responded with a self-deprecating laugh.

'Librarian,' he said, and I looked at him, amazed. To think of it – a real librarian, sitting in our garden over a cup of tea! What could I say to him? There was an uncomfortable silence as I searched my mind for topics. Mozart was my latest passion and eventually I asked the librarian if he knew Don Giovanni, from which I had just acquired a long-playing record of extracts. He looked at me for a moment, eyes wavering, neck wobbling, hands clutching his knees. Then, suddenly he began to speak, almost tonelessly, as though confessing to some dreadful crime.

"Of course it's a conundrum, isn't it – such a perfect work of art, not a note or a word out of place, and yet Mozart feels free to add two arias, just like that, because the tenor asks for them! Purists would cut these arias; they hold up the action, destroy the artistic integrity. But music like *Dalla sua pace* – would you remove such a jewel just because it stretches the crown?"

Having delivered himself of this weighty utterance he stared down sadly into his teacup, a posture which he maintained in silence until his parents emerged from the house. As they were leaving, he turned to me and said, " I hope you enjoy Marlow library. I worked hard on it."

"And will you still be there?" I asked, astonished to have met not only a librarian but a town librarian.

He gave me a frightened look.

"Oh no, I shall be going with them," – he nodded over his shoulder – "to Canada."

"Come along, Ivor," his mother shouted. She was large, formidable looking woman, with permed grey hair and layers of woollen clothing in maroon and mauve. With a nod and a gulp the librarian disappeared into the back of the family car and that was the last I ever saw of him.

But it was not the last of his influence. In those days immigration from Britain was encouraged by the Canadian government, which subsidized the cost. Mrs Deas was able to take her furniture and knick-knacks, down to the last Bambi on the mantelpiece. But, as she explained to my mother, Ivor's books would cause them to overstep the weight limit. So would we mind if they were left behind? If we had no use for them they could always be given to the RSPCA.

The first book that I picked from Ivor's collection was a volume of letters by Rainer Maria Rilke. Needless to say I had never heard of this writer but I was attracted by his name. 'Rainer' had a faraway, exotic sound to it, 'Rilke' suggested knighthood and chivalry. And 'Maria' made me think of a being more spiritual than material who had risen so high above the scheme of things as no longer to possess a sex. I read the book with a feeling of astonishment, just as I had experienced two years before through Bunyan. An air of holiness, a reckless disregard for the world and its requirements seemed to radiate from those mysterious pages. Here was a man who wandered outside society, communing with nature and his soul. I did not suspect that Rilke was a shameless sponge,I could not see that these letters, which seem to be all giving, are in fact all taking, the work of a spiritual vampire. To me they exemplified another and higher mode of being of which I had no precise conception but for which I tried to find a name. 'Aesthetic' sounded right at first; but then 'ascetic' seemed just as good, and somewhat easier to say. Eventually I used both words interchangeably, satisfied that between them they captured the mysterious vision which had been granted to me but withheld from those coarser beings – my parents and sisters for instance – who had no knowledge of books.

Thanks to Rilke I embarked on the aesthetic, or ascetic, way of life. The first requirement was to fall in love with someone pure and inaccessible for whom I could suffer in silence. One of my class-mates seemed a promising candidate. He was handsome, thoughtful, showed a faint interest in music, sought my good opinion. But when I asked him to read Rilke's letters he protested that he didn't have the time. I fixed my eye instead on a girl whom I had seen in Marlow church. She wore a white mackintosh and a white silk scarf, and her neatly plaited hair and cream-coloured cheeks radiated child-like piety. I knew nothing about her except that she came from Marlow Bottom. When I confided this fact to my sister, whose curiosity had been aroused by my ostentatious sighs, she roared with laughter and promptly named the object of my passion 'Big Bertha of Marlow Bottom'. Such taunts notwithstanding, Big Bertha, who was in fact small and delicate, sustained my reading for several months. Then one evening I caught sight of her in a doorway, snogging lasciviously with a man in jeans. I revised my conception of the ascetico-aesthetic life, with love excised from it.

By now I had discovered Dante in the Temple Classics edition, which Ivor Deas had annotated in a fine italic hand. This was my introduction to symbolism. I formed the conclusion that symbols put us in touch with our real selves and that our real selves are vastly more interesting than the pretend-selves we adopt for others' consumption. The theory was confirmed by a reading of Robert Graves's *The White Goddess* – surely the most dangerous way for a child to discover poetry but incomparable in its excitement.

Graves challenged me to read more widely. I began to explore Ivor's other domain, the public library, to whose Eng. Lit. section he had clearly devoted the greater part of his time. All the poets, critics and novelists had found a place in those unvisited rooms, from the windows of which you could see the high wall of a secluded Victorian mansion, occupied, as it happened, by the ageing C. Scott Moncrieff. It was months before I was to know the significance of that name. But the books which Ivor had collected at public expense and which I read, usually four at a time, on a table between the book-shelves, were now inextricably fused in my mind with the view of that high brick wall. Wisteria swarmed over the top of it and a great cedar tree rose in the garden, resting its branches on the coping stones and hiding the house from view. I read like an alchemist, searching for the spell that would admit me to that secret world, where shadows fall on tonsured lawns and the aesthetic (or was it ascetic?) way of life occurs in solemn rituals after tea.

Soon, order of a kind was established in my literary thinking. Thanks to Mr Broadbridge, a Leavisite master, those doing English at A level came to literature only after being steeped in the vinegar of Revaluations. I too, though studying natural sciences, felt the force of Mr Broadbridge's edicts, issued in classrooms three corridors away. Once again, books were divided into those on the syllabus and those off it – the only change being that the syllabus was now indefinitely large. Whatever the charms of Rilke and Graves, they were definitely off the syllabus. Dante was OK, because Eliot said so, but Dante had to be approached through The Sacred Wood and the going was hard. As for Kafka and Kierkegaard, who had also captured my imagination, they were apologists for sickness, tempters who must be banished by those for whom 'life is a necessary word.' The severity of Dr Leavis appealed to me since it made my literary excursions into sins. I went on reading Rilke and Kafka with a renewed sense of being an outsider, obscurely redeemed by the crime which condemned me. And to this day I remain persuaded that it is not life that is the judge of literature but the other way round.

One of the poets on the Leavisite index was a favourite of Ivor's. His copy of Shelley, which I still possess, is annotated in every margin. On its title page is Ivor's name – George Ivor Deas, or Georgius Ivorus Decius as he there expresses it, by way of preface to some lines of Ovid. On the next page, in Ivor's italic hand, is a sonnet, dated 23rd February 1945. It captures, in its stilted way, the premonition that all of us feel when the first enthusiasms of youth begin to wane.

Evolution

In youth he shouts to the stars – "There is no God!"
Laughs till Faith withers in his laughter's flame;
Cries that Law libels Freedom without blame,
That Order sweats and weeps and smells of blood;
Says Life's a dull game played with smudged old cards;
And Death's humiliation no one's gain;
Envies those lunatics who dare be sane
In handcuffs, elbowed on by bored young guards.

Older, with steel of need and flint of fear,
Strikes God ablaze again through bare sky;
Drugs with a sleepy Faith Life's apathy;

Makes hope his soul and Death a doorway near;
Pats Law and Order on their snarling crest,
And lives a meek Assenter with the rest!

The meek assenter who slipped away to Canada at his mother's command, leaving his life behind, was my saviour. Librarians like Ivor made fortresses of books. Taste and scholarship survived there, and could be obtained free of charge. For those born into bookless homes but awoken by chance to literature, the public library was a refuge, a moron-free zone where you could come to terms with your isolation. It was made so by people like Ivor.

I recently had cause to remember him. I had been looking for Wagner's writings from Paris – a collection of wonderful essays and stories, the kind of book that every library should possess, if only to offer a true record of our culture. At last I obtained the book from a dealer's catalogue. On the title page, at the very place where George Ivor Deas would have copied out his name, is a red stamp: 'Discarded by the Hackney Library Services.'

Roger Scruton has published over 30 books, including works of philosophy, literature and fiction, and his writings have been translated into most major languages. His most recent books are a study of Wagner's Tristan und Isolde, *entitled* Death-Devoted Heart *(OUP, 2004)* Gentle Regrets, an intellectual autobiography *(Continuum, 2005)*, Culture Counts: Faith and Feeling in a World Besieged *(Encounter Books, 2007) and* Beauty *(OUP 2009).*

Could we see some identification, please?

Sophie Hannah

I've just read a brilliant book,' I said to my sister on the telephone a couple of months ago. 'You must read it.'

'What's it called?' she asked suspiciously.

'*The Giant's House* by Elizabeth McCracken,' I said. My sister found nothing off-putting in the title so she went on to her next question.

'What's it about?'

'Love,' I said.

'Be more specific.'

'It's about an American spinster librarian who falls in love with an eleven-year-old giant,' I said.

'Oh good,' she said sarcastically. 'I'll be able to identify with it then.'

I was surprised by her reaction. It hadn't occurred to me that she – or the numerous other people to whom I'd recommended *The Giant's House* – might have trouble identifying with the novel because of its subject matter. This was not because all my relatives, friends and acquaintances were giant-loving American spinsters, but because when I read the novel I identified with it so completely that I took it for granted that everyone else would too. The next time I phoned my best friend, for whom I'd bought *The Giant's House* as a

Christmas present, I asked her if she'd read it yet. She had. I asked her what she'd thought of it. 'It was interesting,' she said. 'But very odd.'

'Odd in what way?' I asked.

'Well... I mean, would an intelligent adult woman really fall for a young boy who's a giant?' I couldn't believe it. My friend was displaying clear symptoms of what I had for some years called Peter Coyote Syndrome. I coined the phrase after watching the film *Bitter Moon* with, among other people, my father. In the film a character whose name I can't remember (played by Peter Coyote) falls in love with a young French woman called Mimi, moves her into his flat, and pretty soon gets sick of her and tries to throw her out. She however is so desperately in love with him that she begs him to let her stay, if not as his lover then as his servant. A horrific relationship based on emotional abuse ensues, damaging both parties. I was a bit worried about watching it with my parents because it contained many lurid sex scenes of the none-too-normal variety. When the final credits started to roll and my dad announced that he'd hated the film, I asked him why, thinking I already knew the answer.

'It was just ridiculous,' he said. 'I mean, no-one could possibly feel that strongly about Peter Coyote!'

'What?' I asked, thinking there had to be some mistake. 'Come on, Dad. Maybe you couldn't feel strongly about Peter Coyote, but...'

'Nobody,' he repeated, in a tone that brooked no argument, 'could fall so deeply in love with Peter Coyote. I mean, I could imagine some woman sacrificing her self-respect to be with Paul Newman, or Robert Redford... but Peter Coyote? No way. It's totally unconvincing.' We argued long into the night, but my dad wouldn't budge. In his opinion it was simply implausible that Peter Coyote should inspire in anybody powerful feelings of desire. My mum even chipped in, when I tried to enlist her as a witness for the defence with, 'His teeth were very yellow, weren't they? I think your dad's right, you know.'

Peter Coyote Syndrome is more common that you might imagine. For example, who hasn't, in recent years, heard a comment that closely resembles this. 'Woody Allen's really lost it. He keeps casting himself as the romantic lead opposite young attractive heroines like Helena Bonham Carter and Mira Sorvino. It's ludicrous! As if a beautiful young woman would go for a bespectacled, weedy old man like him.' Allen is, in fact, married to a woman in her mid-twenties who, from the photos I've seen, appears to be far from ugly. And Peter Coyote is presumably married to Mrs Coyote who presumably loves him (I'm just guessing, but you get the point).

When the film *Titanic* came out, some journalists claimed that Leonardo DiCaprio couldn't be taken seriously as a romantic hero because he looked too young, while others said Kate Winslet was too fleshy to be a plausible romantic heroine. What could this be but Peter Coyote Syndrome, the inability to believe that anyone might fancy a person one cannot imagine fancying oneself? Peter Coyote Syndrome is entirely delusional. It has no basis in reality, since in reality the weedy and bespectacled, the fleshy, the young and even the yellow-of-teeth, get fallen in love with from time to time. As I write this article, one of my good friends is pining for a man who (and she would be the first to admit it) looks like a cross between a gorgon and the singer Meatloaf. Try to portray that in a film or a novel though and people would call it far-fetched.

Back to *The Giant's House* then. I should point out at this stage that I am not an American spinster librarian, nor have I ever been in love with an eleven-year-old giant. Why, I asked myself, did I identify so strongly with Peggy Court, the novel's narrator? I came up with two possible explanations, one of which convinced me far more than the other. Here they are:

1) I once worked as an administrative assistant in a private library. I also once fancied a very tall man (although he was forty-eight, not eleven). The combination of these two factors resulted in a certain degree of familiarity. 'Libraries and tall people – that's my sort of thing,' I thought.

OR

2) The opening lines of the novel ('I do not love mankind. People think they are interesting. That is their first mistake.') struck a peculiar, deep chord in me, and I felt as if I might learn something about myself by reading the novel. The combination of naive, unconditional, hopeless love for one person with shrewd perceptive cynicism about people in general felt incredibly familiar and the theme of the novel – love for the outsider, or love for the not-generally-considered-to-be-loveable, and the self-deception that is necessary as a defence mechanism when one's love is unrequited – seemed exactly to mirror my mental landscape at the time.

I hope you've guessed that 2 is the right answer. I think there are various different ways in which we can identify with works of art. The most superficial of these is Prop Identification, in which you identify with the props of a novel or film. Giants, libraries, spinsters – all these are props. This is the sort of identification in which I am least interested. I happen to have curly hair, wear round glasses and drive a green Volvo but I'm not especially keen to read novels about people who have curly hair and round glasses who drive green Volvos. I prefer a deeper kind of identification, where it is the thoughts, feelings and underlying themes that are familiar not merely the props. Therefore I can identify with obsessive love and I don't much care whether its object is an eleven-year-old giant or Peter Coyote or Leonardo Di Caprio or Woody Allen.

I'm not suggesting that my dad's reaction to *Bitter Moon* and my friend's reaction to *The Giant's House* prove that they can only identify on the most shallow level, the prop level. What I am suggesting, though, is that both of them used props as shorthand, when the real failure to identify was deeper, more basic. Both my father and my friend make sensible romantic choices – they are both of the personality type that falls in love with feasible savoury characters rather than impossible unsavoury ones; neither of them has a tendency to fall for misfits, low-lifes or the tragically doomed.

In addition to Prop Identification and Thought/Feeling Identification, I think there is a third kind. It is possible to read a book or watch a film in which neither the superficial details of the characters' lives nor the psychologies of any of the characters are similar to one's own, but where the novel or film is so good, such a powerful work of art, that what you identify with is the artistic endeavour itself. How else would you explain the fact that some of my kindest, least violent friends love *American Psycho* by Brett Easton Ellis?

The other day I was in a bookshop with a friend. She picked up a novel and instantly put it down again, saying, 'I hate it when women write from the point of view of men. It's not realistic. There's no way a man can imagine what it's like to be a woman.' I disagree. There are ways other than the obvious ones, the prop-centred ones, for people to have things in common and good art has the power to expand the imagination, to enable us to get outside ourselves and believe in other people, however unlikely they might seem. If I'd been in Jane Eyre's shoes, I would have said, 'Of course I'll be your mistress – who cares about your bonkers wife in the attic?' I can identify with her reaction, though, because *Jane Eyre* is a work of art, not because I have anything in common with dutiful, virginal governesses.

The word 'realistic' has become a polite way of saying unimaginative. Those who cannot get on with the novels of Iris Murdoch, for example, often say her dialogue is unrealistic. People simply do not, they argue, go up to each other out of the blue and say, 'It is imperative that you allow me to love you. You don't need to say anything now. Just don't say that I can't. You see, you are the force of destiny in my life. I need to be needed by you.' Maybe no-one would say that in real life, but on the other hand, maybe they would. Recently I invited an ex-boyfriend to my book launch. He wrote me a long letter in reply saying that he wouldn't come because the event was taking place at Waterstone's, which retail outlet he described as 'ego-driven and pompous, a 'baseless fabric', an 'insubstantial pageant'. Is it credible that someone could have such strong feelings about what is simply a rather good bookshop? Perhaps not, but it happened.

Furthermore, even if we concede that Iris Murdoch's dialogue does not resemble everyday speech, there is another level on which it could be said to be realistic. I think her great achievement is that she is able to represent states of mind, with all their neurosis and hysteria, in the style of polite, tea-party conversation. Her dialogue may not represent exactly how we speak, but it comes extremely close to representing the ways in which we think, the undignified mental contortions we go through to protect our frail egos. And the sort of dialogue that passes for realistic is as far from the patterns of normal speech as any Murdoch conversation. In reality, most people ramble on endlessly, one fragment of a sentence overlapping with or interrupting another. Editors do not allow that to happen in novels; conversations proceed to the point in an orderly manner with an unrealistically small number of interruptions, stumblings and mumblings.

I am highly suspicious of anyone who attacks a novel or film using a lack of prop identification, or allegations of prop implausibility, as their weapon. Almost always, this shows that they have some deeper, thematic objection to the particular work of art.

This was supposed to be an article about *The Giant's House* by Elizabeth McCracken, and partly, I hope it is. I want to encourage people to read the novel because it's one of the best books I've ever read. (While you're at it, read *The Black Prince* by Iris Murdoch, which is equally outstanding.) But I also want to encourage readers of fiction to broaden their conceptions of what is possible, what is identifiable-with, before we reach the stage where the only novels we can read and believe in are ones about ourselves sitting in chairs and reading.

Sophie Hannah is a bestselling crime fiction writer and poet. Her crime novels have been longlisted for the Old Peculiar Crime Novel of the Year and the IMPAC awards and her poetry collection, Pessimism for Beginners, *was shortlisted for the 2007 TS Eliot award. Sophie lives in Cambridge with her husband and two children.*

De-accessioning

Penelope Lively

De-accessioning is the inelegant euphemism used by librarians. Getting rid of books, they mean. I am de-accessioning right now, a process forced upon me because I have to reduce my living space. I can no longer gaily accession, as I have done all my life, buying, receiving and reluctant to throw out much because one might well want to come back to it at some point. I am now paying for this liberal approach to books. I have far, far too many and there must be some savage culling. So how is one to decide what is essential and what is not?

I have never been a bibliophile, collecting the book as such. A fine edition is welcome if it comes along, but it is content I am after and homely paperbacks will do nicely. Indeed, I cherish many of those for the reading associations they conjure up. The garish, mass-market US paperbacks picked up in early trips across the Atlantic years ago were my first introduction to Willa Cather, Eudora Welty and many other writers. I read that one under a tree on a lobster picnic in Maine... This one reminds me of steamy summer evenings at the home of friends near Boston. That dog-eared copy of Peter Ackroyd's *Blake* kept me sane on an American book tour a few years ago, shunted on and off planes and in and out of hotel bedrooms. On the other hand, I cherish the handsome

1853, calf-bound set of Disraeli's novels (no, I haven't read every one) we bought in Marlborough way back, remembering that autumn afternoon each time my eye falls on the books. And my first Shakespeare is sacrosanct – floppy blue leather binding and print so small I can't read a word of it today. It was a tenth birthday present and I carried it round all day like the Crown Jewels.

The 1883 edition of Macaulay's *Lays of Ancient Rome* is treasured more for its associations than its appearance. I learned by heart out of it at twelve or so and can still recite chunks of 'Lars Porsena of Clusium, By the nine Gods he swore...' But equally, I can never part with a little brown copy, umpteenth reprint, of Vita Sackville West's *The Land* because I remember buying it at about fourteen, following fashion but also trying to start up my own poetry library. In fact, poetry is the easiest area in the de-accessioning process. No need to. Slim volumes, on the whole merciful on shelf-space. The fat *Collecteds* do a bit of damage, but you can get an awful lot of poet into a few feet. I've been a member of the Poetry Book Society for many years, as the best way to keep a regular supply of contemporary poetry coming in and the entire intake probably only fills one shelf. So no de-accessioning of anybody there, thanks be.

It is fiction that is the problem. I have decided on a rough rule of thumb, across the board, fiction and non-fiction alike, which is, am I ever likely to take it off the shelf again? And this at once points up a significant divide. That question far more often prompts a 'no' with fiction than with non-fiction. I didn't care for Gore Vidal's *Creation* first time round, when reviewing it and I'm sure I'll never want to revisit it. On the other hand, that biography of Heisenberg is also gobbling up a good three inches of space and is not a sparkling read but it is full of facts about twentieth century scientific history that I might at some point need. As soon as I start to cull the non-fiction, such arguments present themselves. Here's a biography of William Beveridge – surely that could go? But again it has facts and figures and a bibliography that might come in handy. In the unlikely event that I'm overcome by a sudden lust for a Gore Vidal I can get a paperback. If I am cavalier about pruning the non-fiction I may be depriving myself of a basic reference library, which will mean resorting to libraries elsewhere when I least want to. The existing stock of biography, travel, history, archaeology, popular science and everything else can just about supply me when it comes to looking up fairly straightforward names, dates, facts, figures, arguments and so forth. As soon as I deplete it I shall find I urgently need to know something about the uncertainty principle or the findings of the Beveridge report.

So, non-fiction is nearly exempt. The reject box eventually holds the *Good Food Guide* for 1994, a manual on how to set up and run a plant nursery, (background research for a novel some years back), some outdated travel guides, the history of a publishing house and other similar oddments.

To the fiction shelves, pruning knife at the ready. The most obvious targets are the outsize hardbacks which leap instantly into view, squatting over two or three inches of valuable space. Let's begin here. Vassily Grossman's *Life and Fate* is a whopper. I've started it and given up more than once. But it is a seminal Russian novel, bearing witness to a time and a place. I may yet have another go, more profitably. John Barth's Letters? Not at all to my taste but a central text of twentieth century American literature, one is told. It had better stay. Barry Unsworth's *Sacred Hunger*? Don't lay a finger on that – one of the novels of recent years that I most admire. It could have twice as many inches if need be.

I'm not doing very well. Michael Moorcock? Here perhaps I can be ruthless. I've always struggled with his work and probably won't do so again. So out with something at last. Rohinton Mistry's *A Fine Balance*? I read this with respect but doubt if I shall go back to it. Borderline that, but I'm being far too squeamish already.

Here's a wodge of fat titles by someone I know well and while I'm fond of him/her, I don't much care for his/her work. So that's a real problem. Emotional commitment struggles with expedience, and quite properly emotion wins. The books stay. Mind, this conflict of attitudes about writers and their works can operate to equal effect the other way round. There are several contemporary authors whose books I read with pleasure and admiration but from whom I cross the room if I come upon them in the flesh.

The hefty hardbacks are proving an uncomfortable challenge. Let's abandon them for a moment and go random. Here are a couple of novels by George Macbeth, a far better poet than a novelist. I doubt if I'll read him again so by the rule of thumb they ought to go but I knew and liked him and enjoy his poetry so they have an interest by association and extension. The *Collected Works of Jane Bowles*. Out of this falls a sheaf of notes with page references so I must have reviewed it, way back. Without huge enthusiasm it would seem – 'slithery anecdotes that leave little but a furtive flavour…' But she is highly thought of in some quarters. Far from culling this, I need to have another look and see if I agree with myself.

This raises another problem – one's own shifting relationship with authors. Here's a whole row of Barbara Pym.

Once I read her with appreciation, then went off her altogether and became irritated after half a page. I may yet come round to her once more and curse myself if I've thrown her out. Equally, here's Lawrence Durrell who used to madden me and then acquired a mysterious appeal when I picked up *Justine* last year – what once seemed lush, overblown and portentous now assumed a labyrinthine allure. You cannot step twice into the same book. Or rather, you revisit any book in a different state of mind, with predictable effects. It speaks with a different voice.

This is becoming impossible. I have moved the goalposts. The rule of thumb was that I should eliminate anything I will probably never read again but now I am saying that anything and everything may invite re-reading in the service of one's own mercurial processes of change. We have all been changed by books and must be prepared to change again.

Now these stout spines start to look threatening, each one putting forward a dozen robust arguments for preservation. In the past I have castigated those local authority librarians who were airily throwing out books. Now I feel a sneaking urge to ask them how they set about it. In fact, private and public libraries are two entirely different concepts. The public library caters for all and has an obligation to stock a range of material likely to meet any reasonable demand. But the lesson I am learning in this enforced restriction of fancy is that private reading needs are both infinite and indefinable. Any personal collection of books reflects the shifting tastes and interests of a lifetime. Throwing out any of this is like obliterating some aspect of memory and personality. As soon as it is gone you may feel a sudden urge to reconsider.

In my adolescence I read Harrison Ainsworth and Charlotte M Yonge. There they are still – sombre bindings and dauntingly small print. I look at them with astonishment, doubting that I could get far with either author now and thinking that it must have been a pretty weird fifteen year old who ploughed on and with a certain relish, I seem to remember. To de-accession those titles would be to jettison a slice of my own past. But other teenage reading is long since gone – discarded along the way – Mazo de la Roche, Georgette Heyer, Margaret Irwin – and yet remains in the head still, a distant literary climate. So there is that to remember -books once read float free of their physical incarnation.

But it is the book glut that is at issue right now and about which something has to be done. At moments a random cull is tempting. Every fifth title; beginning and ending of the alphabet – out with Amis, Atwood, Austen, Wells, Woolf, Wharton. Ultimately, the only thing to do is to soldier on with this rational but inoperable system of considering each book as a possible future need. Why have I got it in the first place? Have I read it and if not am I likely to do so? Is it important sui generis? Is it important to me? Boldly remove the book from the shelf... and then, as like as not, put it back again.

Penelope Lively grew up in Egypt and settled in England after the war. She is the author of many novels and short story collections for adults and children. She has won the Booker Prize for her novel Moon Tiger, *as well as the Carnegie medal and the Whitbread award. In 2001 she was awarded a CBE. She is a regular contributor to a number of newspapers and literary journals.*

Visiting the store-room

Francis King

When I was an Oxford undergraduate, I once accompanied Ian Robertson, a friend and future director of the Ashmolean Museum, into the Museum's basement store-room. With us was Willy King, one of the great ceramic experts of the day. King (no relation) at once began to dash excitedly hither and thither, calling out to us as he unwrapped now one object and now another: 'Take a look at this! Just take a look at this! Magnificent! Why isn't it on display?... And just look at this! Look!' I feel the same about novels of the recent past, already consigned to a metaphorical storeroom even though, on average, they seem to me to be in no way inferior to the novels now on display in the literary pages of newspapers, on television arts programmes and in the windows of booksellers.

Certainly it is true that the novels of today, when compared with the novels of the recent past, are amazing for their technical proficiency, often achieved by writers still in their twenties and even their teens; but to make such a comparison is like comparing CDs of the vocal stars of our own times with old '78s of such singers as Melchior, Supervia or Schumann. There is no doubt that the former will always win on the quality of their recordings; but equally no doubt that the latter will all too often win on the quality of the singing.

Somerset Maugham once remarked to Terence Rattigan that, with luck, a dramatist could expect his vogue to last for fifteen years. Maugham himself, of course, did better than that. In 1908 he had four plays running simultaneously in London; in 1932 his penultimate and, in the view of many, best play *For Services Rendered* was widely acclaimed; and even today the heir to his estate, the Royal Literary Fund, is munificently supported not merely by his literary but also by his dramatic royalties. But, in general, his statement is sadly true – as is at once evident when one considers the decline in popularity, and therefore in the number of performances, of such once acclaimed playwrights as J.B. Priestley, John Osborne, John Arden and Arnold Wesker in the recent past, and John Galsworthy, John Van Druten, Dodie Smith and Rodney Ackland in the period immediately before them.

The vogue of a novelist lasts on average for about twice as long as that of a dramatist. I see two reasons for this. Firstly, a play, unlike a novel (unless, of course, it is by Ivy Compton-Burnett), depends for its effect almost entirely on its dialogue, and there is always an interval between the time when dialogue, on the verge of becoming old-fashioned, has the dry, musty taste of a cake just past its sell-by-date and the time when it recedes yet further back, to achieve the distinction of being savoured for its vintage flavour. Secondly, once a dramatist begins to go out of fashion few producers will mount productions of his or her work, since they will be terrified of not being able to attract sufficiently large audiences for financial success to be assured. But whereas thousands and thousands of people must be attracted to a play for it to be commercially viable, in the case of the re-issue of a book only a thousand or so are necessary.

The happiest novelists who pass out of vogue are those, like Hugh Walpole, May Sinclair and Francis Brett Hart, who do so in the aftermath of their deaths, the unhappiest those, like Charles Morgan, Henry Green, Angus Wilson, John Braine and John Wain, who do so while still living. Looking back on a lifetime of novel reading I often experience a sense of desolation as I think of these and other writers who, though they have now passed out of vogue, not merely gave me intense pleasure at my first reading of them but continue to do so even today, when, as increasingly often, I take down one of their books from my shelves.

My most recent experience of this was with Edith de Born's *The Bidou Inheritance*. As when the author presented me with a copy of the book some twenty years ago, my first astonished thought after devouring a single page was 'How beautifully this woman writes!' Why astonished? The answer to that is that Born was an Austrian, who married a Frenchman and lived much of her life in Belgium but, like Conrad, Nabokov and Julian Green, she miraculously wrote better in her adopted language than most people in the language to which they were born. My second, much later thought was that she dealt with the cupidity of the French bourgeoisie with all the vividness of a François Mauriac or a Julian Green. In general, English novelists, unlike Born, have little interest in property and money – Galsworthy and C.P. Snow were exceptions – and they therefore rarely understand them. Barely twenty years have now passed since the death of this agile and subtle writer. But when I mention her even to well-read friends, they usually frown, shake their heads and either say that they have never heard of her or murmur something like 'Yes, the name vaguely rings a bell.'

Another novelist whom I can always re-read with delight is C.H.B. Kitchin, close friend of L.P. Hartley and in my view the better, because the more reliable and more balanced, novelist. Even in his lifetime he was known chiefly as the author of a best-selling detective novel *Death of My Aunt* – 'that wretched book', as he would call it, though, along with his other books in the same genre, it brought him in far more cash than his 'serious' works of fiction. Hartley described Kitchin, who was as adroit at extemporising on the piano and gambling on the stock exchange as at constructing marvellously ingenious plots, as 'the most talented man I have ever known.' Kitchin's *The Book of Life* has a similar theme to Hartley's far better known *The Go-Between* and is, in my view, a book no less fine.

There was a time at the beginning of my career as a writer when, shamefully, I experienced a pang of envy on seeing that a book by Jocelyn Brooke had yet again received a lead review from some such highly influential critic as Raymond Mortimer, Cyril Connolly or David Cecil, exerting an influence on readers of a potency that no critic achieves today. Before his death in 1966 I learned that Brooke had been unable to find a publisher for his latest and, as it sadly proved, last novel. As literary adviser to Weidenfeld and Nicolson I then tried to persuade George Weidenfeld that the firm ought to take him on. His response was a rueful 'I'm afraid his day is over.' But when last December a Christmas bout of 'flu gave me the opportunity of re-reading Brooke's semi-autobiographical trilogy, *The Military Orchid* (1948), *A Mine of Serpents* (1949) and *The Goose Cathedral* (1950), in which he recalls his childhood, school and army days with a teasing, tender mixture of comedy and poignancy, I at once became totally convinced that he still had a glowing day ahead of him, somewhere in the future.

Other semi-forgotten writers who give me as much pleasure now as they did when first I came on them, are a quartet of short-story writers from whom, when still a novice, I learned an enormous amount about the art of the short-story – L.A. Manhood, T.O. Beachcroft, Malachi Whitaker and William Sansom. I react in similar fashion to re-readings of a number of half-forgotten novelists. The foremost of these to come to mind are Forrest Reid, much admired by his friend E.M. Forster, John Cowper Powys – in my heretical opinion a greater novelist than D.H. Lawrence, whom he resembles in his loquaciousness and his rhapsodic hymning of the glories of sex. Eric Linklater, whose often critically ignored or patronised later books are as good as, or superior to, his wildly lauded early ones. L.H. Myers, whose inter-war philosophical trilogy *The Near and Far*, set in India at the time of the Mogul Empire, had the rare distinction of being one of the few contemporary works of fiction to earn the whole-hearted approval of F.R. Leavis, and Joyce Carey, who, such was the frenetic vigour of his imagination, would often work on some half-dozen of his remarkable and astonishingly diverse books at one and the same time.

Allan Massie, a novelist happily and deservedly still in vogue, once wrote to me: 'The room at the top gets narrower as the years pass – and there is room for only a few older writers on the platform.' If there is little room for older writers, then there is virtually none for recently dead ones unless they are of the stature of Maugham, Forster and Greene. For me this room at the top resembles the consulting room of a harassed GP. There are all those older folk, patients of many years, demanding the GP's attention, but should he not, the GP asks himself, focus that attention exclusively on the youngsters impatiently crammed into the waiting room who still have most of their lives ahead of them and who are desperate to have their turn?

There is, it might be argued, a rough fairness in opting to

deal chiefly or even solely with those youngsters, but there is also, inevitably, a sadness.

Francis King, former drama critic of the Sunday Telegraph *and now fiction reviewer for* The Spectator, *has published more than forty books. His latest novel,* Dead Letters, *has recently appeared in paperback. He is now at work on another novel.*

Learning to read, Yorkshire 1928

Kit Pyman

'Put on 'Tea for Two' my mother said.

Like a terrier down a rabbit hole, I dived into the cupboard where the records were kept, piles of them in dusty brown covers with coloured central discs, that I knew as well as my own hand. I emerged breathlessly with the right one, and placed it on the turntable.

'There,' cried my mother. 'Fancy being able to read at four!'

I made the mistake of boasting about this. Next time I was asked, my oldest brother silently produced two new records which I was totally unable to identify and I was mortified.

I also had the habit of 'reading' books which I knew by heart to family visitors and he played another of his schoolboy tricks by substituting a different book.

This event precipitated such a storm of tears that my mother agreed that I should join the schoolroom group, on condition that I sat at the end of the table and didn't interrupt. I sat mouse-like watching them make their writing scrawls and found to my amazement that I could make scrawls too. We used the phonetic method. Laboriously copying out letters I mouthed ah, buh, cuh, duh, eh – and some of the simpler groups of letters actually formed themselves into words – c a t and m u m.

Now, when the family straggled out for a walk I practised my new skill. 'Bell End' was achievable with difficulty, but the next strip of letters, carved out of wood and nailed to a low wall was a different matter. Guh, Yi, Sss, Yi? My tormentor told me that this particular Guh was pronounced Juh – and the writing said Gypsy Lane. I was overwhelmed with a deep sense of injustice at this phonetic treachery and collapsed with my face pressed to the sign like a tragic heroine. The rest of the family had the usual paddle in the ford and visited the *Fat Pig* and on the way home another brother heaved me on his shoulders.

'Never mind' he said, 'reading's a rotten bore'.

In the calm of the hall I saw a flushed and tearful face in the mirror, with a faint G branded on the left cheek.

We children had to rest every day after lunch. Once, my Aunt Moira's blue eyes and blonde shingle appeared round my door and she tossed me a big book with a picture on the front of a horse drawing a cart. I sat up against the pillows and propped it on my knees. By dint of skipping wildly, and swinging my head swiftly from left to right at every word of more than four letters, I managed to get the drift of the text. I found myself at the end of the allotted hour tensely holding the book open at page thirteen! Even now I can feel the glow of astonishment and achievement that enveloped me.

After that I found words everywhere. When my mother took me to meet my grandmother at the department store in town, I suddenly realised that the curly golden pattern across the frontage was not just decoration, but must surely say 'Dickson & Benson'. As we walked up the stairs, a board at the top said 'Mannequin Parade today'. I did my special head swing from left to right. Now this was something I knew about, – little men in green suits. 'Do they really have manikins here?' I asked my mother.

'Oh yes' she said. 'Nearly every week'.

I determined to keep an eye out for them, but meanwhile we had reached the children's department. There was a notice at the counter where my mother was talking to the assistant. 'Jaegar' it said. I felt rather strange. Never had it occurred to me that jaguars might haunt Dicksons & Bensons. They might even be quite large, and they were certainly supposed to be fierce. I looked around. Everything seemed calm. My mother held a vest against me. I indicated the notice. 'How big are they?' I whispered.

'Size?' she said. 'Well, they come in assorted sizes, of course'. I trod closely in my mother's wake as she walked through the swing doors into the white and gold glory of the café. Forgetting the jaguars for the moment, I raced across and flung my arms round my grandmother, who had established a bridgehead at one of the larger tables. The pink linen cloth reflected warmly on her beloved face, her fur coat was tossed on one chair and her parcels on another and her plumed hat sheltered us both as she swooped over to kiss me.

My mother caught up and told her about my 13-page excursion into *Black Beauty*. Overflowing with congratulations, Granny dipped a heavily ringed hand into her bag and brought out half a crown. Half a crown! My weekly pocket money was threepence. It occurred to me that reading might be even more rewarding than I had imagined. She placed me on the chair next to her, and listened with deepest interest while I read the menu, only helping me with 'Iced Fancies'.

Friends and relations joined our table and a general hubbub arose above me while I inhaled my fizzy lemonade. Bubbles of pleasure streamed along my veins and induced a state of memorable euphoria, although I knew in my heart that somewhere manikins marched and jaguars (in assorted sizes) prowled about in the shadows. Reading, I discovered, had its darker side.

Kit Pyman was a regular reader of, and occasional contributor to Books and Company.

O, the books of my youth

Juliet Nicolson

In childhood, books absorbed more of my conscious thinking than the real world, because they were my real world. Magical occurrences did not seem remote -to me they were a likelihood. Imagination was rooted for me in the real world, and books blurred beautifully the edges of dreary reality.

At home there is a box hedge and when I turn the corner and am caught almost unawares by that nutty smell I have a profound sense of being again the six year old who looked for the door to my own secret garden. I expected any day to discover the hidden back panel in the spare room wardrobe which would lead me to Narnia. My first nightmares featured the vanishing grin of the Cheshire cat, and I would dream of boating down the distant thick waters of the deliciously dirty Great Grey Greasy Limpopo River.

Leaving behind me the pre-school world of free-wheeling imagination, I was unusually fortunate in having four teachers who, in successive schools, gave me an increasing awareness of the riches I might discover in books.

The first was the as-yet unpublished novelist, Penelope Fitzgerald. She taught me English when I was about seven. Perhaps the germ of the idea for her first book was even then on her mind but her students were aware only that she sat on the desk, an act of such informal daring by a teacher that we were aghast. We were captivated by Mrs Fitzgerald as, swinging her legs, red curls escaping from her chaotically pinned bun, she read us terrifying and knitting-phobic stories of the tricoteuse, skewering Dicken's *Tale of Two Cities* forever into our imaginative landscape.

At her memorial service in London, many decades later, a deeply evocative recording of her voice was played, returning me for those few moments directly to my childhood classroom.

At boarding school the second teacher, Mrs Innes-Crump, was the implausibly named inspiration of my early adolescence. She 'performed' (it is the correct word to describe the drama of her delivery) *Gray's Elegy*, pince-nez hanging from her neck on a silver chain, her bosom heaving with enormous emotion, as she led her students through the gathering gloom of the country churchyard.

At A level college in London, my tutor was Norah Banks. Unable to walk far, owing to a cruel childhood illness, she taught from home and each week I would go to her house for my solo tutorials. She lived at the very end of the Jubilee tube line and travelling for an hour alone in the smoking carriage, on my way to discuss Samuel Beckett's novels, seemed to me the apogee of sophistication. Norah wore cleavage-challenging T-shirts, introduced me to black coffee and during the break would play me her latest Miles Davis record on the gramophone. Through Norah I discovered D.H. Lawrence. I swooned over Ursula's passion for Anton in *The Rainbow*, and was enthralled by the legitimacy of having a conversation with a teacher about sex.

At Oxford, Anne Wordsworth, the fourth of these early muses, taught in a falling down shed at the bottom of a garden in North Oxford. Teetering piles of books, half a bottle of wine, and Rizla papers littered the floor. There was an old sofa in the corner covered in a frayed, beaujolais-red shawl. It all seemed impossibly and irresistibly decadent. To her I owe a lifelong passion for Yeats, the ability to quote long chunks from Shakespeare's *Antony and Cleopatra* and an understanding of the novels of Virginia Woolf. Mrs Wordsworth's (surprisingly, I was never invited to use her Christian name) infectious delight in the skywriting scene from *Mrs Dalloway* remains with me still. The over-quoted lines in Tennyson's memorial poem to his friend Hallam, 'Tis better to have Loved and Lost than never to have Loved at all' always recover their original poignancy if I return to the context in which I first read them in that garden shed.

And I discussed with her the dilemma of my own first love- two suitors, but which to pick? Following her instinctive advice, I spurned the gift of silver hooped earrings from the first, in favour of the inscribed copy of Jon Stallworthy's selection of *Love Poetry* left on my doorstep by the second.

The concentration of talent at the publishing company where I worked after leaving university was considerable. Proof copies I would take for homework reading included William Boyd's first novel, *A Good Man in Africa,* Peter Ackroyd's fairy tales inspired by Oscar Wilde, a biography of Milton by A.N. Wilson, *The Old Patagonian Express* by Paul Theroux, David Niven's memoir *Bring on the Empty Horses* and an outrageous story in pictures by Raymond Briggs revealing that Father Christmas ate snails on holiday. Unwittingly, I realize now, I was among the first privileged readers of books that have become modern classics.

Later, working in New York in the publicity department of Grove Press, my job included making arrangements for the playwright Arthur Miller to read from his autobiography *Timebends.* Such was his fame that in order to accommodate his many fans, no less a venue than the Carnegie Hall was chosen. I sat among a spellbound audience as he read his description of his courtship of Marilyn Monroe.

'She had taken on immanence in my imagination, the vitality of a force one does not understand, but that seemed on the verge of lighting up a vast surrounding plane of darkness'.

Afterwards, as he signed copies of his book, I took my turn in the queue. When I reached the top, as he momentarily turned away from me, I picked up his spare biro, and put it in my pocket. Despite having read to the un-lovely end of this particular love-story, I could not resist stealing the pen which had been held in the hand of the man who had once been married to Marilyn Monroe.

Places associated with great literary figures are almost as powerful as the words themselves. To be in the room at Chawton, beside the tiny writing desk where Jane Austen wrote *Emma,* or to stand quite alone in the unaltered bedroom in Rome where Keats died are profound experiences. I remember an irrational excitement in finding myself unexpectedly driving through East Coker in Somerset and realizing that T.S. Eliot had named one of his *Four Quartets* after this village. Terrified, when camping one night with my brother in the orchard at Rodmell, where Virginia Woolf's ashes are buried, I like to think I sensed her ghostly genius hovering among the apple trees.

Books have always sustained me. During the summer that my mother was dying, I read *Anna Karenina* for the first time. My total absorption in the story of one woman's passion and tragedy was a great antidote to my own sadness.

I am uncertain whether I will ever read that novel again, as it is so powerful a reminder of a time to which I am not anxious to return, but it was for me then the sublime proof that literature can provide a sustaining life-giving escape from reality.

More often though, I choose to go back to writing that is well known to me. I find huge pleasure in watching a new production of *Hamlet.* The anticipation in hearing the soliloquies is as delicious as the moment before locating the exact source of an itch. *Le Grand Meaulnes* will always be my private symbol for the yearning for an exquisite but perhaps unrecoverable experience. I love the occasional and sudden understanding of the beauty of the words of an over- familiar hymn, of a glimpse into a significance and a poetry of which I have been previously unaware.

Looking through the list of set texts for the A. Level English literature syllabus, my heart skips. I realize that I now have a legitimate excuse to spend time re-reading *The Great Gatsby* and *Othello* on the convenient premise that I would like to be of some constructive help to my student daughter. I want to be able to contribute a little more than a rusty comment on the nature of jealousy, the green-eyed monster or a half remembered allusion to Daisy's voice full of money. So I have taken these books down from the shelves. But if I am truthful, this re-read is an excuse to re-visit not only these favourite texts themselves but a younger carefree me.

I love knowing that those pages will always be there to return to, like the black bin bag containing unstuck-in photographs, or old love letters. The pages of the edition of *Tess of the D'Urbevilles* that I last read when I was nineteen or my undergraduate heavily-annotated collection of Eliot's early poems, smell like youth bottled.

My father used to read *Wuthering Heights* once every five years, and was rarely without a Jane Austen novel beside his bed. Castaways on *Desert Island Discs* rarely choose new books but take old friends to sustain them in that lonely place. When absolute certainties are challenged, whether it be the permanence of a previously indestructible skyscraper or the assumed foreverness of a deep friendship or when it is simply the fear of time itself passing, it is of unfathomable reassurance to know that books and words cannot ever be taken away and that the box-hedge moment is always there, should I choose to go and seek it out.

Juliet Nicolson is the author of two books, The Perfect Summer *and* The Great Silence *that tell the true story of life before and after the First World War.*

Corpses in the quad: the curious case of Oxbridge crime

Andrew Taylor

In *The Case of The Missing Three-Quarter,* Sherlock Holmes remarks to Dr Watson, 'I think we must run down to Cambridge together. All the indications seem to point that way.'

In the geography of crime fiction, the indications have continued to point to Cambridge – and to Oxford – ever since. For nearly a century the two university towns have loomed large in the fictional landscape of the United Kingdom. Only London can surpass them as a setting for murder and mayhem. Even today they have crime rates of epidemic proportions.

Moreover, their inhabitants have a longstanding appetite for crime fiction. In 1983 Livia Gollancz, whose firm published so many Oxbridge-flavoured detective novels, said that most of Gollancz's hardback crime fiction sales, apart from those to public libraries and in London, were in Oxford or Cambridge.

These two universities are not the only locations for crime fiction set in institutions of higher education. The academic mystery has a long and varied tradition on both sides of the Atlantic. After all, the detective and the scholar have a common goal, the search for truth, and many of their techniques from the use of reason to the collection of evidence, have obvious similarities. But for nine out of ten readers the label 'academic mystery' brings to mind punt-laden rivers, gilded youth and dreaming spires. And of course another corpse in the quad.

Oxbridge crime fiction is a rich and complex field and this article is no more than a sort of aerial survey of some of its landmarks. There are a number of questions that spring directly from it. What is the nature of the fascination Oxbridge holds for crime writers? Has it changed over the years? Is it possible to distinguish the two universities from one another in fiction as well as in fact?

Appropriately enough, even the origins of the universities are shrouded in mystery, with hints of fraud and murder attached. In the past each has claimed to be older than the other – as one authority has remarked, 'the oldest of all inter-university sports was a lying match' One story claims that Oxford was founded by King Mempric in the days of the Prophet Samuel. Another assigns the foundation of Cambridge University to that well-known Spanish prince, Cantaber, in the fourth century. To reinforce these impressive credentials, Cambridge also claimed to have a charter from King Arthur (dated 531 AD) and to have founded the university at Oxford at the command of King Alfred.

A more plausible story links the early history of the two universities with murder or possibly manslaughter. In 1209, it is said, an Oxford student killed a woman of the town during a drunken brawl. The townsfolk rioted and lynched several students. King John closed down the university. There followed a great migration of masters and scholars to Cambridge. When Oxford re-opened, some of them stayed in their new home. In other words a corpse in Oxford may have led to the foundation of Cambridge.

Enthusiasts have frequently discussed whether Sherlock Holmes was educated at Oxford or Cambridge. It is commonly agreed that he must have gone to one or the other, though Conan Doyle himself (educated at Edinburgh) is silent on this point. The evidence is circumstantial and inconclusive. Some of it involves learned debate over Conan Doyle's use of the words 'quad' and 'court', which are Oxford and Cambridge terms respectively. Dorothy L. Sayers triumphantly unearthed a T.S. Holmes who had studied at Sidney Sussex College, Cambridge, in the 1870s, but her case was undermined when the historical Holmes proved to have been the Chancellor of Wells Cathedral rather than the world's foremost consulting detective.

The fictional connection with Oxbridge takes a variety of forms. Some crime stories are set there. Others are suffused with what might be called the Oxbridge spirit – their characters carry the flavour of common room and quad into the outside world. Sarah Caudwell's witty crime series, which began with *This Was Adonis Murdered* (1981), is set in legal London, but her books are thoroughly Oxonian in tone if not in setting. In a typical running joke Cantrip, one of the recurring characters, is constantly being reminded by the others that he had the misfortune to be educated at Cambridge.

A third category uses Oxbridge as an essential part of the CVs of their characters – usually to imply brains, breeding or both. According to Ian Fleming, for example, James Bond found time from other commitments to gain first-class honours in Oriental Languages at Cambridge. In Lauren Henderson's wise-cracking, ultra-cool *Freeze My Margarita* (1998), the plot revolves around a production of *A Midsummer Night's*

Dream and most of the characters seem to have known one another at Cambridge.

For many people, the label 'Oxbridge Crime' conjures up the cosy college whodunnit written between the wars. J. C. Masterman's *An Oxford Tragedy* (1933) was one of the earliest of these. Michael Innes's first detective novel, *Death at the President's Lodging* (1935), set at a fictional university but thoroughly Oxbridge in all but name, shows how witty and intellectually tortuous such novels could be – and how mannered to the point of self parody. Here is Innes's protagonist, Inspector Appleby, lecturing an admiring colleague who lacks the benefit of an Oxbridge education:

> 'The bones were abstracted from Australia – by no irrational ferrety, as Sir Thomas says. They were snatched from the pious care of an aboriginal posterity to gratify the scientific proclivities of one Johnnie Haveland.'

Glyn Daniel's *The Cambridge Murders* was published in 1945 but set in the 1930s. His 'Fisher College', with its two great courts much admired by Ruskin, stands between Trinity and St John's, a miraculous feat of compression given the twenty-feet gap between the two colleges. The author gives as much attention to matters gastronomical as he does to his plot. For Daniel, as for Waugh in *Brideshead Revisited,* a world war had cast a rosy glow over the culinary achievements of the uncertain years of peace preceding it. (Nostalgia in some shape or form is a feature of many Oxbridge crime novels. It is noticeable that the characters in Michael Innes's later novels, written and set in the 1980s, often act, speak and think in a manner more appropriate to the 1930s.)

Masterman, Innes and Daniel were Oxbridge dons, as

were a number of other crime writers of the interwar period, including Ronald Knox and G. D. H. Cole. But in Oxbridge, as elsewhere, crime fiction before World War II was more varied and less cosy than it is often assumed to have been. One bizarre example is *Darkness at Pemberley* (1932) by a youthful T .H. White, better known as the author of *The Once and Future King*. It is an extraordinary fusion of the donnish detective novel (almost before it had been invented) and the thriller in its most exuberant, Edgar Wallace mode.

As a crime novel – as any sort of novel, *Darkness at Pemberley* is a failure but an endearing one. At 'St Barnabas College', there are no fewer than three murders, each equipped with its own sketchmap. The Master is a cocaine addict. One of the fellows is a pusher. Another don, who has 'tenacity of a viper' and is further distinguished by his 'trilling chuckle', coats the toothbrush of an intended victim with diphtheria germs. The book works its way towards a Grand Guignol climax at Pemberley, the ancestral home of Jane Austen's Darcys (the neighbours have ostracized the current head of family since his conviction for drug smuggling).

Margery Allingham's *Police at the Funeral* (1931) is another Oxbridge novel which fails to fit the Golden Age stereotype. True, her detective Albert Campion is at this point in his career a blend of Wooster and Wimsey. But the story breaks new ground in its structural ingenuity – in its time, it must have been as startling as Agatha Christie's *Murder of Roger Ackroyd*, and Allingham anticipates the development of the crime novel by being as much interested in her characters as her plot. The story revolves around the Faradays, formerly a great academic dynasty in the Huxley/Darwin mould, who live under the tyranny of the ruthless widow of a college

Master. The university looms on the periphery of the story, and family politics are at the centre of it.

No consideration of Oxbridge crime would be complete without a mention of Dorothy L. Sayers' *Gaudy Night* (1935), the third of the four novels which describe the relationship between Lord Peter Wimsey and Harriet Vane. It is a crime novel without a murder. In *Bloody Murder*, Julian Symons gives it short shrift – he says it's 'essentially a 'woman's novel' full of the most tedious pseudo-serious chat between the characters that goes on for page after page.' This verdict seems grotesquely unfair to women in general and to Sayers in particular. Symons points, with more justification, to the book's snobbery and to the 'breathtaking gap' between Sayers's 'intention and achievement.'

But if the novel was a failure by Symons' standards, it was surely an honourable one. Sayers deserves credit for straying beyond the unadventurous confines of the Golden Age puzzle mystery. She tried to use a detective story both as a vehicle for serious themes – the value of scholarship, and the price it exacts – and as a novel of character and manners with an attendant love story. It is a book that has given some of its readers their first glimpse of the intellectual excitement a university can offer – including, as it happens, Jill Paton Walsh. (Paton Walsh was the Booker-shortlisted author who, more than sixty years later, completed *Thrones, Dominations,* the Wimsey-Vane novel that Sayers left unfinished years before her death) Finally, *Gaudy Night* has not only entertained and stimulated readers for over sixty years, it has also encouraged crime writers to experiment with the genre in their turn.

It was perhaps inevitable that after World War II Oxbridge

crime fiction should have been bedevilled by a longing for vanished securities. Such nostalgia was not uncommon elsewhere but it lasted longer in Oxbridge. Institutions that measure their lives in centuries are by their very nature reluctant to welcome sudden change. Women were not admitted to degrees at Cambridge until as late as 1948.

The best crime writing of this period was written to amuse – and it still does. Many of the post-war novels of Michael Innes were witty and humane, among them *The New Sonia Wayward* (1960) and the thriller *The Journeying Boy* (1949). Edmund Crispin brought a streak of inspired lunacy to the solemn matter of detection. In *The Moving Toyshop* (1946), for example, a toyshop moves around Oxford in an apparent contravention of the laws of physics. Detection is left in the wilfully unsafe hands of Gervase Fen, Professor of English Literature. In *Buried for Pleasure* (1948) the solving of crime is elbowed aside by the sharply satirical comedy of Fen standing as a candidate in a Parliamentary by-election, and by the cameo role of the non-doing pig.

These entertainments, however, had less successful imitators, them Robert Robinson's *Landscape with Dead Dons* (1956), a grimly farcical Oxonian detective story, and the five Dr Davie novels by V. C. Clinton-Baddeley. To be fair, *Landscape With Dead Dons* was very well received when it was published and fizzles with youthful energy. (It contains more naked men than any crime novel I know.) But on the whole it hasn't aged well.

Youthful energy does not characterize Clinton-Baddeley's novels. The books are so slow-moving that it seems a distinct possibility that they were written when the author was half asleep. Dr Davie is an elderly Cambridge scholar who takes his creature comforts as seriously as the crimes he is called upon to solve. In *My Foe Outstretch'd Beneath the Tree* (1968), the final pages are reserved not for the revelation of the murderer's identity but for something far more important to the author – a detailed recipe for crème brûlée. Gourmandising, incidentally, is an important motif in the Oxbridge crime novel of this period. Murder might be fun, you feel, but food was serious.

The last of the Davie series was published in 1972. In complete contrast the same year saw the appearance of P. D. James' fifth novel, *An Unsuitable Job for a Woman*. The book brings a welcome dash of reality to Oxbridge. A well-known microbiologist hires private detective Cordelia Gray (in her first recorded case) to investigate the suicide of his only son, a Cambridge undergraduate. The result is not only an excellent crime novel but also one which succeeds in relating the university to its surroundings. This was a sign of changing times. In the past many Oxbridge crime novels treated the surrounding town as a below-stairs appendage to the university – a source of college servants, pubs, tobacconists and socially undesirable girls.

Since the 1970s, Oxbridge has continued to appeal to crime novelists. By and large they have followed what might be called the donnish pattern. In Anthony Appiah's *Avenging Angel* (1990), set in Cambridge, even the anonymous letters are written in Latin. But most writers have been more willing to come to terms with the modern world than their immediate predecessors were. Norah Kelly has written two novels showing the same university from the viewpoint of a resolutely unenchanted Canadian academic – *In the Shadow of King's* (1984) and *Bad Chemistry* (1994). Before her collaboration with Sayers, Jill Paton Walsh produced two crime novels of her own, *The Wyndham Case* (1993) and *A Piece of Justice*

(1995), whose heroine is a Cambridge college nurse with a life outside the university.

Oxford has also provided the setting for a crop of interesting crime novels in the last few years. Two of them – Hazel Holt's *The Cruellest Month* (1991) and Veronica Stallwood's *Oxford Exit* (1994) – include corpses in the Bodleian Library, which is clearly not a safe place for scholars in the late twentieth century.

Oxford backgrounds also characterize two interesting oddballs. Gwendoline Butler's superbly atmospheric *A Coffin for Pandora* (1973) takes us back to the 1880s. Michael Dibdin's *Dirty Tricks* (1991) brilliantly explores undesirable behaviour in a more recent setting. In both these novels, the focus is on the town rather than the university. Another variant is Ian Morson's Falconer series, beginning with *Falconer's Crusade* (1994), which is set in medieval Oxford. Brother Cadfael, you might think, has tracked down Inspector Morse.

Morse brings us to one of the most substantial landmarks in the literature of Oxbridge crime. Colin Dexter's Morse series has now, thanks to television, done for Oxford what Bergerac did for the island of Jersey. The first Morse novel, *The Last Bus to Woodstock,* appeared in 1975. Dexter carefully avoids the academic and social snobbery which disfigured so many Oxbridge novels in the past. He himself was educated at Cambridge, which perhaps accounts, at least in part, for his ability to avoid over-identification with Oxford University. He gives us the advantages of the dreaming spires (and don't they look nice on television?) but none of the drawbacks.

'Would Rotherham (for all I know, a splendid town),' Dexter once wrote, 'have made as suitable a stage for Morse and the murders he is sent to solve? I doubt it.' So do we.

Morse is a man who straddles boundaries: university and

town, Wagner and real ale – he offers something for everyone. He matriculated at Oxford but left without taking a degree. The long-suffering Lewis is much more than a stooge: like Watson, he helps to bring a Great Detective down to the level of mere humanity. It is significant that Dexter's plots are set in a world where academic life is only one element among many.

The same can be said of Elizabeth George's *For the Sake of Elena* (1992), set in Cambridge. The story opens when the undergraduate daughter of a high-flying history lecturer is battered to death while jogging beside the Cam. The fictional college is not entirely plausible and nor is its relationship with the university. The book poses unintended problems for British readers, partly because the detective is a belted earl from Scotland Yard. Both the dialogue and the view of the British class system seem to owe more to Hollywood than to life. The characters are strong, passionate and twisted – though marred by their tendency to lapse into Californian psychobabble in unguarded moments. Nevertheless this is a strong, well-plotted book which exploits to the full the melodramatic possibilities of a dank Cambridge winter. Like Margery Allingham and P. D. James, Elizabeth George is not a graduate of the university – her perspective is that of a well-disposed but not uncritical outsider.

Another characteristic of the Oxbridge mystery through the decades has been its Oxbridge-educated author's barely concealed delight in his own cleverness. A recent example is *The Poison Tree* (1997) by Tony Strong. Set among no doubt typical university folk in Oxford, it is a strongly-flavoured confection of violence, sex, and post-modernist lectures on detective fiction. The book is not to everyone's taste but it is undeniably powerful, assured – and often fun as well.

Perhaps it is best considered as a satire -Michael Innes Goes Noir. If nothing else it shows that Oxbridge crime fiction is continuing to evolve vigorously into the next century while retaining its links with the old.

There is no question that Oxbridge has played a significant role in the development of crime fiction in this country – and no question, either, that the two university towns are continuing to inspire writers.

It is tempting to argue that Oxbridge crime fiction over the last seventy-odd years can be divided into three stages. In the 1930s, the accent was on variety and experiment. The period immediately following World War II saw a flight from reality towards nostalgic fantasies, often with rococo plots, written to amuse, flatter and reassure their middle-class readers. From the 1970s onwards, however, there has been a steady shift into a bleaker, more realistic world where the universities are part of a wider social context. The plot of a modern Oxbridge crime novel often has more in common with the Nine O'Clock News than it does with the elegant diversions of the corpse-in-the-quad school. But the settings still work a little of their old, comforting magic on the reader. These phases of development are of course an oversimplification – no more to be relied on than the facile assumption that a greater degree of realism is necessarily a sign of literary maturity.

Why does Oxbridge have this stranglehold over the imaginations of so many crime writers? The obvious explanation is that many crime writers have been to university at Oxford or Cambridge, or have other connections with those cities. In practical terms, Oxbridge offers many advantages to the plot-hungry crime writer – the universities are conveniently close to London, they are crammed with a wide variety of interesting people of many nationalities, they are centres of power and wealth – and, of course, cradles of genius. Oxbridge still has a certain glamour, a volatile compound of architectural splendour, social status and academic excellence. Both cities are centres for international tourism and look well on television. In short, they are a crime writer's paradise.

Can Oxford and Cambridge be usefully distinguished from each another in terms of crime fiction? This is a more difficult question to answer. Oxford's contribution to the genre is almost certainly larger and more varied. The Oxford crime novel is often more smugly intellectual than its Cambridge counterpart – Dorothy L. Sayers' Oxford, for example, is portrayed as little short of the Celestial City. It could also be argued that Cambridge crime novels have tended to be more experimental in form, less snobbish and more open to external influences in their content. But these are gross generalizations and they should be treated with the suspicion such generalizations deserve.

It is clear though that Oxbridge has a deep-rooted attraction for readers as well as writers. For some the two universities still represent an ideal – something valuable and unique in a world of pre-stressed concrete and mass-produced minds. Others are simply curious about the ancient nests of academics and the strange activities which are pursued there. Like Harrods and the monarchy, Oxford and Cambridge have snob appeal, and like warm beer and cricket, they are a part of England's image of itself, and of its image abroad.

For all these reasons, and more, crime fiction set in Oxford or Cambridge has an enduring appeal. Though the deerstalker is rarely worn in contemporary Oxbridge, it's a safe bet that corpses will continue to decorate the quads and courts of the twenty-first century.

P.C. Plod apprehended

Andrew Taylor

The literary significance of Mr Plod has often been underestimated. To be brutally frank, it is usually overlooked altogether. It is more than time to rectify such a glaring omission.

Recently a magazine sent me one of those flattering author questionnaires – flattering because it seems incomprehensible that anyone other than yourself should be interested in such unanswerable questions as why you write fiction or where your ideas come from. The magazine took me by surprise by asking what was the first book I could remember reading by myself.

It is an imaginative question. I can remember literally scores of stories that were read to me before and after I learned to read. I can also remember, though only vaguely, the first story I limped through with the help of someone older and wiser. It was in a reading primer and the principal characters were John and Mary; nothing else remains in the memory except the intoxicating sense of triumph, even power, conferred by the skill I had mysteriously acquired.

But the real milestone was the first book I voluntarily read – and endlessly re-read – by myself. I had no difficulty in finding the answer to that question. It was Enid Blyton's *Hurrah for Little Noddy*, published in 1950 and the second title in what eventually became a 24-book series and much else besides. This was the true beginning of a lifelong addiction to the printed word in general and fiction in particular.

I still have my much-scarred copy complete with luridly effective illustrations by Beek and the politically-incorrect garage-owner Mr Golly. (Mr Golly has been removed from modern editions in a high-minded literary version of ethnic cleansing. It still puzzles me why it should be politically incorrect to have a golliwog as a local plutocrat and employer – you could argue that the reverse was true.) When as an adult I re-read the story, I realised that it contained at least a partial answer to another question – why I eventually became both a reader and a writer of crime fiction. *Hurrah for Little Noddy* is nothing if not a crime novel writ small.

For the benefit of those who grew up beyond the reach of junior British literary culture, Noddy is a wooden puppet with a colourful dress sense and the emotional development of a determined if slightly retarded four-year-old. Having arrived in Toyland in volume one of the series, Noddy is faced in volume two with the grim necessity of earning a living. After a spot of spring cleaning at a dolls' house, he lands a temporary job washing cars at Toy Garage. At home one evening, Noddy discovers he has left his hat at work. Later that night he goes to fetch it, only to find that a gang of goblins is stealing the cars. Commandeering an old banger, Noddy tails the convoy of stolen vehicles. After a 60 mph chase by moonlight, the old banger crashes. Noddy is rescued by his friend Big-Ears the brownie, who happens to be passing – for reasons Enid Blyton does not go into.

When Noddy returns to Toy Village, the 'chief policeman' (who becomes PC Plod in later volumes) arrests him for the theft of the cars because his hat has been found in the empty garage. Noddy is banged up in a cell and left to rot. Fortunately Big-Ears reappears at this point. He has traced the cars to an underground garage at Goblin Town and demands that Noddy should not only be released but rewarded. The police raid Goblin Town, recover the cars and impose a punitive fine on the entire community (one penny per goblin). Noddy is rewarded with a car of his own and the Toy Village equivalent of a civic reception.

Misinterpreting the significance of Noddy's hat is the first of PC Plod's forensic blunders in the series. Plod plays an important part in the affairs of Toy Village, though no one could accuse him of being a member of its intelligentsia (in this he resembles Noddy himself). He is not unkind but he is an inflexible and reliably stupid figure of fun, given respect only because he is imbued with the formidable power of the state.

I had to wait thirty years for the later adventures of Mr Plod, until my own children had entered the intense but relatively brief Noddy phase of their development. No aficionado of the infant roman policier should miss *Mr Plod and Little Noddy* (Number 22, 1961). Mr Plod falls from his ladder while painting the police station and is confined to hospital. This is an altogether delightful experience for him, as Noddy discovers when he visits the bedridden police officer:

Flowers were on the table beside him, a box of chocolates, five new books, his favourite cigarettes, and a bottle of lemonade! He was even wearing a nice paper helmet that kind Mrs Tubby Bear had sent him...

'Hallo, hallo,' he said to Noddy... 'I tell you Hospital is a LOVELY place to come to. I can't imagine why some silly people are afraid of going there. It's as good as a holiday – better, because everybody gives you presents.'

Perhaps Mr Plod was delirious, or the cigarettes did not contain ordinary tobacco. Meanwhile, Big-Ears assumes the powers of a Special Constable and takes control of Toy Village. Noddy, far from being criminalized by his wrongful arrest in Volume 2, sets himself up as a one-man CID Department. When two bicycles are stolen from Mr Golly's Garage (where security continues to be lax), it is Noddy who recovers the stolen goods and immobilizes the thieves until a posse from Toy Village can arrest them. ('I shouldn't be surprised if Big-Ears doesn't give you a good whipping,' Mr Tubby Bear, leader of the posse, tells the villains.)

Mr Plod is delighted because this means he can stay longer in hospital. 'Noddy is very naughty sometimes, Big-Ears, but he's very very good at heart, isn't he?' The incompetent and in this case powerless police officer has come to appreciate the value of an amateur investigator. In its essentials the scene occurs in many adult crime novels.

When she gave Mr Plod these characteristics, Enid Blyton gave a childish form to an adult stereotype already established in British crime fiction for more than half a century. She also implanted the stereotype, no doubt unknowingly, in the youthful and receptive minds of a new generation of British crime writers. Her influence has travelled beyond literature – in some circles 'the Plod' has become a slang synonym for the police.

The ultimate responsibility for the birth of Plod probably rests with Conan Doyle. Earlier fictional policemen tended to be forcefully intelligent and often enigmatic figures – think of Inspector Bucket in Dickens's *Bleak House* and

Sergeant Cuff in *The Moonstone* by Wilkie Collins. But an omniscient 'consulting detective' could not reasonably be expected to co-exist with competent police officers capable of mounting effective criminal investigations – hence Inspector Lestrade and most (though not quite all) of the policemen with whom Holmes has dealings. Holmes's success made the birth of Plod inevitable.

Lestrade and Co came into being because there was a technical need for stupid police detectives. Without them Sherlock Holmes would have been out of a job. In the twentieth century, there was an additional reason for police detectives to have low IQs. British crime writers unwittingly introduced the NQOCD Factor into their work. This wholly regrettable novelty dominated the way police officers were portrayed for more than a generation.

NQOCD is a snobbish acronym, now a historical curiosity. It is usually said to stand for "Not Quite Our Class, Dearie." In terms of crime fiction, it really gets under way after the end of World War I. In a sense the classic English whodunnit of the 1920s and '30s was an escape from an intolerable reality – an escape, in other words, from the consequences of the First World War

As far as crime fiction is concerned, two of these consequences are particularly relevant. The first, which perhaps it had something to do with the second, was memorably summed up by Reginald Hill (of whom more later). On one occasion a lady asked him why the majority of the great British crime writers of the Golden Age were women. "Madam," he replied, "because all the men were dead."

The second consequence was the sudden rise in popularity of the dashing gentleman sleuth, most of whom were created by women authors, and the corresponding decline in status of police officers. Readers were increasingly invited – and increasingly willing – to admire sleuths, not just because of the work they did but also because of their social standing. Some crime novels of the period are designed to reassure and flatter as well as entertain. Their secret message is that the rich man is still in his castle and the poor man is still waiting for scraps at his gate and wouldn't dream of joining the Labour Party, so all's well with the world.

The underlying assumption of these novels was that both authors and readers were on the same elevated level as the aristocratic sleuth. The implication is that we too can smile with discreet and impeccably well-bred amusement at the funny accents and naive attitudes of the lower classes and all foreigners. We too know instinctively how to handle servants and vintage port – firmly on the one hand and gently on the other. Here we have crime fiction as wishful thinking.

For modern readers the best of such novels can be enjoyed as well-constructed literary diversions. They also have a period charm – and of course they allow us to feel agreeably smug. They let us dabble in anthropological pleasures (just as *Pride and Prejudice* gives modern readers a glimpse of upper class courtship rituals two hundred years ago). It is interesting to speculate about which qualities in contemporary fiction will seem either educational or unintentionally hilarious to our grandchildren.

But how does all this relate to police officers in crime novels? Because if the sleuth is a gentleman amateur, then according to this standard it follows that policemen, who are paid for what they do, are by definition inferior. Hence P.C. Plod.

Despite this crushing drawback, police officers were still necessary in crime novels written between the wars and for two reasons. The first is that even the grandest of sleuths has to have some contact with the machinery of the law – people to do the menial and unglamorous work of fingerprinting the suspects, pursuing enquiries in inconvenient places, keeping the handcuffs in their tunic pockets, conducting the post-mortems etc.

Secondly, police officers have an aesthetic purpose in the crime novel of the Golden Age -they are designed to throw into greater relief the talents of the sleuth, just as Watson does for Holmes. Someone has to pursue the red herrings. But the role of Golden Age police officers is much more complicated than Watson's was. As well as being dim-witted, they must accentuate the other virtues of the gentleman sleuth. That means police officers must be of a lower social class – and often rather crudely comical so that well-bred smiles may flicker occasionally across the finely chiselled features of the gentleman sleuth and the sophisticated reader.

All this amounts to a generalization and there are many exceptions to it. Agatha Christie is not a particularly good example of the syndrome, for the simple reason that she is insufficiently snobbish. Perhaps this is one reason why her books have lasted so long and been translated so widely. Neither of her main protagonists is a police officer. One is a silly little foreigner; the other is an old maid living in the country. When police officers appear, they are not exactly realistic but on the whole they are not sneered at either. Miss Marple's friend Inspector Craddock becomes so friendly with her that he calls her Aunt Jane.

Dorothy L. Sayers took a different approach. With Lord Peter Wimsey and Inspector Parker, she created the classic example of the relationship between gentleman sleuth and police officer. Parker's face is described as 'plain, though pleasant' in *Strong Poison*, an excellent whodunnit with the bonus of considerable emotional impact. Parker's origins are lowly and Non-Conformist. He has a comical if inexplicable taste for theology, particularly that of the early church. Parker's NQOCD Factor diminishes over time, largely because of the elevating influence of Wimsey's friendship. Indeed, he is eventually sucked into the upper classes when he marries Wimsey's sister, but even when gentrified he remains properly conscious of his station in life. Wimsey treats him firmly but with great affection, as if Parker were a favourite dog. And like a dog, Parker needs to be told what to do.

In *Whose Body*, for example, Wimsey has to leave London. He summons Parker and gives him a string of orders:

'I want you to take this [letter] to Scotland Yard immediately and get it sent out to all the workhouses, infirmaries, police stations, YMCAs, and so on in London... I want to know whether any man answering that description has been taken in anywhere, alive or dead, during the last fortnight. You will see Sir Andrew Mackenzie personally and get the paper sent out at once, by his authority... you will ask him to have men in readiness with a warrant to arrest a very dangerous and important criminal at any moment... When the replies to this paper come in you will search for any mention of St Luke's Hospital or any person connected with St Luke's Hospital, and you will send for me at once.

'Meanwhile you will scrape acquaintance – I don't care how – with one of the students at St Luke's. Don't march in there blowing about murders and police warrants, or you may find yourself in Queer Street. I shall come up to town as soon as I hear from you...'

☆

Admittedly Wimsey was suffering from a nervous breakdown at the time but even so, it must be wonderful to have such God-given natural authority. Sometimes though, Parker shows signs of being less than grateful. In *Murder Must Advertise* he is mistaken for Wimsey, brutally assaulted and nearly murdered. Not unnaturally he feels a little peeved about this. But Wimsey wastes no sympathy on him. He tells Parker he's 'uncommonly lucky to be alive, and ought to be jolly well thankful instead of grumbling...' This witty and often underrated novel also gives a sharply satirical glimpse of bohemian life in London and an insider's view of the advertising industry. It proves once and for all that Dorothy L. Sayers had a sense of humour.

Wimsey is a prime example of the species of gentlemen sleuth now, for better or worse, nearly extinct. Some Golden Age crime novels had a professional sleuth, a police officer, on centre stage but in many cases this was less of a departure than it might appear. Some of the novels were no more than dramatized puzzles, like those of Freeman Wills Crofts, whose Inspector French is little more than a pipe-smoking thinking machine attached to a digestive system. Others – which oddly enough have lasted better – did nothing to rehabilitate P.C. Plod, they simply allowed the gentleman sleuth to masquerade as a police officer.

Ngaio Marsh's novels provide one of the best examples. One scene is repeated over and over again in her books – a character's surprise at meeting Detective Inspector (later Superintendent) Roderick Alleyn for the first time. In *Overture to Death,* Alleyn is talking to the squire and the squire's son Henry comes to rescue his father. Henry fears that the policeman 'will carry his bowler in with him and his boots will be intolerable... A mammoth of officialdom!' Imagine his surprise when he finds someone who looks like one of his father's friends – 'an extremely tall man, thin and wearing good clothes, with a air of vague distinction…' who reminds Henry of a 'grandee turned monk'.

Alleyn's brother is a baronet, and in many ways the Inspector is indistinguishable from Wimsey or Marjorie Allingham's Campion – he too has a good tailor, a degree from Oxbridge, a flat in the West End and a manservant. And he also has his NQOCD sidekicks. Chief among them is Inspector Fox, usually referred to with dreadful and relentless whimsy as 'Brer Fox'. Even Alleyn's murder cases seem made to measure. In *The Nursing Home Murder* the Home Secretary dies in suspicious circumstances. Naturally it is Alleyn who is called in – after all, he was at school with the Home Secretary's brother-in-law.

Ngaio Marsh created a sub-species of gentlemen sleuth in a series of crime novels where the characters and settings are almost always more interesting than the crimes and the investigations. (The first third of a Marsh novel is almost always the best and usually bears re-reading.) Michael Innes went one better and created a sub-species of the sub-species. John Appleby is the donnish variant of the gentleman sleuth masquerading as a police officer.

A typical example of a novel which displays Appleby's unique talent is the splendidly convoluted *Hamlet, Revenge*. A member of the government, the Lord Chancellor, is murdered while playing the part of Polonius in an amateur production staged at the country home of the frightfully posh Duke of Horton. To make matters worse a top-secret document has vanished, as so often happens in this sort of novel. The Duke immediately reaches for the telephone. Thirty-five minutes later, when Appleby saunters back to his London flat from the ballet, he finds the Prime Minister and the Commissioner of Metropolitan Police waiting eagerly for his return. Only Inspector Appleby, it seems, has the requisite forensic and literary-critical skills for a case of this gravity, and of course there's no danger of social solecisms upsetting the delicate equilibrium of a ducal house party. There's even a fire engine parked outside Appleby's flat, ready to whisk him to the scene of the crime – because, rather endearingly, the Prime Minister thinks fire engines have nicer sirens than police cars and earn more respect from the travelling public.

The best Applebys are almost as improbable as an episode of *Cracker* but far more fun. For police work at its most surreal, it's hard to beat *Appleby on Ararat* and *Appleby's End*, though *Stop Press* runs them close. Unlike Alleyn, Appleby doesn't take himself seriously.

PC Plod, however, was biding his time. Even during the 1930s, there were glimpses of police officers who were more than figures of fun or puzzle-solvers with attendant corpses. Simenon's Maigret showed the way. The plot of *The Madman of Bergerac* is melodramatic to the point of absurdity but the characterization and the sense of place are not. Maigret and his cases are located in a world which is palpably, often painfully, real.

In this country Josephine Tey's detective, Inspector Alan Grant, is a transitional figure. Plod struggles like an unlovely butterfly to emerge from the chrysalis of the gentleman sleuth. Tey's eight novels all bear re-reading – the only pity is that there are so few. Grant appears in five of them. In the earliest, *The Man in the Queue*, Grant's debt to the gentleman sleuth is most evident – he has private means, good manners and handmade shoes.

But Grant is much more than this. We have the satisfying

sense that there's more to him than his creator chooses to reveal. He makes mistakes both as a man and as a police officer. In *To Love and Be Wise,* he learns a painful lesson about what it is to be grown up. Grant is a recognisable human being who wins our sympathy not because he's nice or clever or witty but because (as Auden said of Yeats) he's silly like us.

Tey's intelligence and moral seriousness underpins her books, which are never dull – even when Grant spends an entire novel lying in a hospital bed and investigating the murder of the Princes in the Tower during *The Daughter of Time.* In Tey's last book, *The Singing Sands,* the murder seems oddly incidental. What lingers in the memory is Grant's struggle against claustrophobia and his fear of sliding into a nervous breakdown.

In the last fifty years, PC Plod has steadily improved his station in life. There are many reasons for this, among them the influence of American crime fiction, the erosion of British class distinctions, a taste for documentary realism nourished by film and TV and an increasing demand for psychological realism. But this has been a gradual process. If a random sample in the UK were asked to name the three best-known contemporary British detectives in crime fiction, it is a safe bet that the most popular choices would be P.D. James' Adam Dalgliesh, Colin Dexter's Morse and Ruth Rendell's Wexford.

True, these are all police officers and they operate in far more realistic settings than their pre-war equivalents. But each has something in common with his genteel predecessors. Dalgliesh is a poet, a man of refined tastes, Morse is a former Oxford undergraduate, a devotee of crosswords and Wagner and Wexford's range of reading commands his readers' respect and astonished admiration.

PC Plod in his late twentieth-century form is better enjoyed elsewhere. Here are three of the many available versions – chosen not at random but because they have given me particular pleasure. They illustrate, incidentally, that the lot of the modern fictional policeman may be no happier than that of his predecessors but it is certainly more varied.

The most cheerful of the three is Inspector Purbright who appears in most of Colin Watson's Flaxborough novels. At times he seems to be the only sane inhabitant of the town which gives the series its name ('A high-spirited town... Like Gomorrah'). Purbright appears first in *Coffin, Slightly Used* and plays a greater or lesser role in ten more books. Some of them work better as comedies than as crime novels but good comic crime writing is so rare that it would be churlish to cavil.

Watson produced sharply effective crime novels peopled with a varied cast of eccentrics. He pokes fun at their antics with a genial savagery that oscillates between dirty postcard humour and Waugh-like wit. His targets range from espionage and black magic to marketing and undertaking. An organic form of Viagra can be found in *The Flaxborough Crab*, the brainchild of one of crime fiction's most appealing villainesses, Miss Lucilla Edith Cavour Teatime. Without Purbright, the series might have tipped over into farce. He is more than a policeman, he is the reader's solitary reference point. This Plod is not a figure of fun. In Watson's world, he is almost the only character who isn't.

Other authors have taken Plod abroad and given him a different nationality. His most common destination is Italy. Magdalen Nabb and Donna Leon have both created memorable Italian policemen, in Florence and Venice respectively. My personal favourite is Michael Dibdin's Commissioner

Aurelio Zen, an amiable moral vacuum who first appears in *Ratking*, which centres on a kidnapping case in Perugia. Zen is more concerned with retaining his job than with solving murders. For him truth is a private luxury that sometimes has little to do with the official results he provides.

Zen has since appeared in several novels, variable in quality but all beautifully written. He drifts in a cloud of Nazionale cigarette smoke through a densely observed modern Italy. *Dead Lagoon* is set in a darkly plausible version of modern Venice and offers a bleak insight into the dangers of revisiting one's past. Perhaps the most enjoyable is *Cosi Fan Tutte*, which reworks Da Ponte's libretto in the form of a crime novel set in modern Naples.

Finally, the quest for Plod should return to England and examine – or rather, relish- the Dalziel-and-Pascoe novels of Reginald Hill. The series began with *A Clubbable Woman* in 1970, and has grown steadily better. Superintendent Dalziel and Inspector Pascoe of the Mid-Yorkshire police, are now finding a wider audience through television. The blunt Dalziel with his Rabelaisian appetites is a constant contrast to the university-educated Pascoe with his left-wing wife and his awkward conscience.

Hill's books are much more than well-crafted whodunnits with a provincial setting. Most of them explore issues springing naturally from their plots, from pornography to the growing of roses. Hill is also excellent on communities and how they work. He writes with great wit (which only occasionally degenerates into facetiousness) and an impressively clear-headed compassion. His police officers are neither idealized nor demonized, though perhaps it is just as well that Andy Dalziel is unlikely to be found outside Mid-Yorkshire.

It is hard to recommend individual titles from a series

which has been so consistently good. If you haven't read these novels before, there is much to be said for beginning at the beginning and going on until the end. My personal favourites are *Underworld,* with its grim echoes of the Miners' Strike, *Bones and Silence,* which takes place against the production of a cycle of Mystery plays and the haunting *On Beulah Height,* with its drowned village, its music and its dead children.

As Dalziel and Pascoe so clearly show, PC Plod has outgrown his tormentors. No longer a figure of fun, he can rub shoulders on equal terms with Inspector Bucket and Sergeant Cuff. Perhaps the changes he has undergone have less to do with him than with ourselves. In one sense Mr Plod holds not a truncheon but a mirror. Crime fiction, old and new, provides the police officers its readers desire.

Andrew Taylor's novels include the bestseller, The American Boy, *the* Roth Trilogy *(filmed for TV as* Fallen Angel*) the* Lydmouth Series, Bleeding Heart Square *and his latest book,* The Anatomy of Ghosts. *He has won the Diamond Dagger of the Crime Writers Association and is the Spectator's crime fiction reviewer.*

The country of the pointed firs

Penelope Fitzgerald

The author of the novel *The Country of the Pointed Firs*, Sarah Orne Jewett, born in 1849, was widely read at the turn of the century, much less after the First World War. Now, perhaps, she will be read again.

Sarah Orne Jewett was a New Englander, descended from a well-to-do merchant family in South Berwick, Maine. Her father was a doctor with a local practice (although he later became Professor of Obstetrics at Bodouin), and she was brought up as one of an extended family in the 'great house' of her grandfather Jewett in South Berwick. It was a place of hospitality where she could listen to the stories told at leisure by visitors, among them superannuated sea-captains and ship owners and relatives from the lonely inland farms.

As a child she was not a great scholar, preferring hopscotch, skating and her collections of woodchucks, turtles and insects. 'In those days,' she wrote, 'I was given to long childish illnesses, to instant drooping if ever I were shut up in school,' so that her father, trusting in fresh air as a cure, took her with him on his daily rounds, teaching her at the same time to keep her eyes open and telling her the names of plants and animals. He recommended her to read, in her teens, the poetry of Tennyson and Matthew Arnold, Sterne's *Sentimental Journey*, and Milton's *L'Allegro*. Her mother and grandmother advised *Pride and Prejudice*, George Eliot's *Scenes from Clerical Life* and Harriet Beecher Stowe's *The Pearl of Orr's Island*.

In 1867, Jewett graduated from Berwick Academy with serious thoughts of studying medicine. The echo of her debate with herself can be heard in her novel *A Country Doctor*. Nancy Price – 'not a commonplace girl, – has been left alone in the world. Her guardian is the beloved country practitioner, Dr Leslie, whose principle is 'to work with nature and not against it.' He believes the wild, reckless little girl is born to be a doctor and he turns out to be right. Although, on a visit away from home, she meets a young lawyer to whom she is in every way suited, she gives him up. In the face of criticism from nearly everyone in her small-town community she goes back to her medical training.

Jewett herself never had to face the test of society's disapproval. She gave up the idea of becoming a doctor simply because she was not well enough. Rheumatism became a familiar enemy, tormenting her all her life long. A legacy from her grandfather meant that she would never have to earn a living and she decided against marriage, perhaps because she felt she was not likely to meet anyone to match her father. But her writing, which had begun with small things, stories for young people, occasional poems, and so forth, had become by 1873 'my work – my business, perhaps and it is so much better than making a mere amusement of it as I used to.'

Like so many great invalids of the nineteenth century, Jewett continued with amazing fortitude to travel, to make new friends, to move according to the seasons from one house to another. Wherever she went she answered letters in the morning and wrote in the afternoons. For twenty years she spent the summer and winter months with Mrs Annie Fields; (it was one of the close friendships known as 'Boston marriages') and spring and autumn in 'the great house' in South Berwick, making time, however, for trips to Europe to meet pretty well everyone she admired. In July 1889 she visited Alice Longfellow (the daughter of the poet) at Mouse Island, in Boothbay Harbour, Maine. This was her first visit to the district of the 'pointed firs' She made several more in 1896, when her novel *The Country of the Pointed Firs* appeared, first as a serial in the Atlantic Monthly and in November from the publisher Houghton Mifflin.

This short novel is her masterpiece, no doubt about that, but it is difficult to discuss the plot because it can hardly be said to have one. Dennett's Landing is a 'salt-aired, white-clapboarded little town' on the seaboard of eastern Maine, more attractive than the rest, perhaps, but much like them. 'One evening in June, a single passenger landed upon the steamboat wharf.' She is a writer who has taken lodging in the town, in search of peace and quiet. Her landlady, Mrs. Elmira Todd, is the local herbalist, being a very large person, majestic almost, living in the last little house on the way inland. In a few pages Jewett establishes forever the substantial reality of Dennett's landing. We know it, we have been there, we have walked up the steep streets and we taste the sea air. Now we have got to get to know the inhabitants, slowly, as the narrator does herself and, in good time, to hear their confidences. Jewett knew all about fishing and smallholding and cooking haddock chowder, about birds, weather, tides and clouds. She had a wonderful ear for the Maine voice, breaking the immense silences. She quotes more than once what her father said to her – 'Don't write about things and people. Tell them just as they are,' and she understood the natural history of small communities, where you will find impoverished, lonely people, often old but proud, self-respecting and respected.

The narrator of *The Country of the Pointed Firs* rents the local schoolhouse, for fifty cents a week, as her study. Here her first visitor, apart from the bees and an occasional sheep pausing to look in at the open door, is Captain Littlepage, an ancient retired shipmaster. His reminiscences are not what we expect. He tells a story of the unseen – a voyage west of Baffin Island which fetched up 'on a coast which wasn't laid down or charted' where the crew saw, or half-saw, the shapes of men through the sea-fog 'like a place where there was neither living nor dead.' These were men waiting between this life and the next. Captain Littlepage offers no further explanation and indeed it' is generally felt in Dunnets Landing that he has overset his mind with too much reading, but Mrs Todd, with a sharp look, says that 'some of them tales hangs together tolerable well.'

Loneliness and hospitality are the two extremes of the hard existence on the coast of Maine. Elijah Tilley, one of the old fishermen, thought of as a 'plodding man' has been a widower for the past eight years. 'Folks all kept repeating that time would ease me but I can't find it does. No, I just miss her the same every day.' It is his habit to lapse into silence. What more is there to say? Towards the end of her life, Sarah Jewett gave some words of advice to the young Willa Cather. 'You must write of the human heart, the great consciousness that all humanity goes to make up.' Otherwise it may remain unexpressed, as it often does in Dunnett's Landing.

Joanna, Mrs Todd's cousin, was thrown over by her fiancé and withdrew to live by herself on thirty-acre Shellheap Island, 'a dreadful small place to make a world of'. She had some poultry and a patch of potatoes. But what about company? She must have made do with the hens, her one-time neighbours think. 'I expect she soon came to making folks of them.' But Joanna maintained the dignity of loss. She lived, died and was buried in Shellheap Island. We are in a world where silence is understood.

When the time comes for the narrator to leave, Mrs Todd, who has become a true friend, hardly speaks all day, 'except in the briefest and most disapproving way.' Then she resolutely goes out on an errand, without turning her head. 'My room looked as empty as the day I came... and I knew how it would seem when Mrs Todd came back and found her lodger gone. So we die before our own eyes, so we see some chapters of our lives come to their natural ending.'

Jewett is an expert in the homely and everyday who gives us every now and then a glimpse of the numinous. (That, perhaps, is why Rudyard Kipling wrote to her about *The Country of the Pointed Firs*, 'I don't believe even you know how good that work is.') She does this, for instance, in a short story, *Miss Tempy's Watchers*. Upstairs lies the outworn body of kindly Miss Temperance Dent, while in the kitchen two of her old friends, keeping vigil before the next day's funeral, gradually nod off. 'Perhaps Tempy herself stood near, and saw her own life and its surroundings with new understanding. Perhaps she herself was the only watcher.' In one of the later Dunnetts Landing stories, *The Foreigner*, Mrs Todd observes 'You know plain enough there's something beyond this world – the doors stand wide open.' There are moments, too, of communication or empathy between friends which go beyond human understanding. Friendship, for Sarah Orne Jewett, was the world's greatest good.

On 3 September 1902, her 53rd birthday, she was thrown from her carriage when the horse stumbled and fell. She suffered concussion of the spine and never entirely recovered. 'The strange machinery that writes' as she described it 'seems broken and confused.' For long spells she was in fact forbidden by her doctors to read or write, which must have been a cruel deprivation. In 1909 she was back in South Berwick, where she had the last of a series of strokes, and died in the house where she was born.

Penelope Fitzgerald was a biographer and novelist. Her 1979 novel, Offshore, *won the Booker prize, and she was a frequent contributor to the* London Review of Books. *Her final novel,* The Blue Flower, *was published in 1995. Winner of The American National Book Critics fiction prize, it was widely considered to be her masterpiece. She died in 2000.*

The Brontë sisters

Lucasta Miller

The story of how the Brontës first got into print is one of the enduring tales of literary history. Three sisters, daughters of a Yorkshire clergyman, scribble in secret for years until, led by the eldest, they determine to publish their efforts. Living in an age which they perceive to be prejudiced against women writers they decide to use the ambiguously gendered pseudonyms Currer, Ellis and Acton Bell. Their first book – a jointly written volume of poems – is a commercial disaster- only two copies are sold. But when Charlotte's *Jane Eyre* reaches the bookshops in 1847 it becomes an instant bestseller. Emily's *Wuthering Heights* and Anne's *Agnes Grey* follow, and the mysterious Bells soon become the talk of the town.

Anyone wanting to build a representative bookshelf on the Brontës should begin with their novels. This may seem obvious but the sisters have been so celebrated for their lives that their works – which are, after all, the reason why they became famous in the first place – have sometimes taken second place in the popular imagination. It is more than a century and a half since 'Jane Eyre fever' first hit literary London but Charlotte Brontë's classic novel has lost none of its original freshness. It is, as one early reviewer put it 'a book to make the pulses gallop and the heart beat.' Those reading it today for the first time are just as likely to feel overwhelmed by its extraordinary intensity as Thackeray, who found himself so caught up in the new novel that he missed a deadline and was found in floods of tears by his astonished servant.

Charlotte Brontë's tale of a poor governess who eventually marries her employer, but only after his mad first wife has perished in a dramatic conflagration, is at bottom a fairy-tale, its basic plot deriving from *Cinderella* and *Bluebeard.* This mythic structure is fleshed out with a highly original mix of Gothic melodrama on the one hand and detailed naturalism on the other. But the true secret of the novel's force was described in 1848 by the leading critic G. H. Lewes (George Eliot's future partner) as 'its strange power of subjective representation.' Jane Eyre is probably the most appealing first person narrator in literature – the reader cannot help but identify utterly with her voice, and her passion and emotional honesty are irresistible.

In this regard, *Wuthering Heights* is totally different from *Jane Eyre.* Conceived as a tale-within-a-tale – what critics have called the 'Chinese box effect' – it does not invite us to offer our unreserved trust to its awkward narrator, Lockwood, nor even to Nelly Dean, the servant who tells him the history of Cathy and Heathcliff. Those whose preconceptions of Emily's disturbing novel derive from its Hollywood image as the archetypal story of romantic love may be as shocked as its first readers were by its scenes of casual violence and psychopathic cruelty and perhaps surprised by its terse economy of style which is as far from purple prose as you could get. Critics will never reach consensus on this enigmatic work but anyone wanting to know the latest academic views should have a look at a collection of essays in Macmillan's *New*

Casebook series. Emily's lyric poetry is as stunning as her novel and the 1999 Penguin edition is particularly worth having.

Re-interpreted in numerous guises, from poems, plays and comedy sketches to an unfortunate Cliff Richard musical and a Kate Bush pop song, *Jane Eyre* and *Wuthering Heights* have achieved cult status and become woven into the fabric of popular culture. This is not the case with the Brontës' other novels, which are less easily reduced to basic mythic formulae. Anne's *Agnes Grey* and *The Tenant of Wildfell Hall* together with Charlotte's *The Professor* (written before Jane Eyre but published posthumously) and *Villette* and *Shirley* are not as widely read today as they deserve to be.

Villette is Charlotte Brontë's masterpiece, but it is not a comfortable read. Matthew Arnold found it 'hideous, undelightful, convulsive.' Unlike the open-hearted Jane Eyre, its narrator, Lucy Snowe, hardly puts you at your ease – she conceals vital information from the reader and offers blatantly misleading interpretations of her own behaviour. Most of what we can infer about her happens beneath the surface of the narrative as the recurring images of burial suggest. This is a novel of the unconscious mind whose phantasmagoric imagery, at times luridly surreal, reflects an uncompromising portrayal of mental disintegration which was groundbreakingly original at the time it was written. Based on Charlotte's own experiences as a pupil and teacher at a school in Brussels, *Villette's* autobiographical aspect – including a desperate visit to a Roman Catholic confessional – makes it particularly unsettling. Lucy Snowe describes the 'creative impulse' as 'an irrational demon'. How far is Charlotte Brontë in control of the psychological forces she uncovers?

The Professor is also based on Charlotte's Brussels experience. The difference is that the narrator is a man, whose voice is less compelling than those of Jane Eyre and Lucy Snowe. Nevertheless, in the heroine, aspiring teacher Frances Henri, Charlotte addresses feminist issues of women and work in a startlingly modern light. *Shirley* – which suffers structurally from the fact that Charlotte broke off writing it in the middle to nurse her sisters, both of whom died before she took it up again – also engages with social issues- the industrial revolution and the role of women.

Anne Brontë is something of a Cinderella, having never achieved as much recognition as her elder sisters (In *Withering Looks,* a satirical two-women show which played a few years ago at the Drill Hall Theatre, London, she is always just off stage, having popped out on some putative errand. When she finally appears it is in the diminutive form of a glove puppet.) But status has been raised by feminist criticism which has at last acknowledged the sophistication with which both her novels address questions of how children are conditioned into conventional gender roles. *Agnes Grey* was based on her own experiences as a governess (the Penguin edition has a particularly good introduction by Angeline Goreau which considers Anne's relationship to her elder sisters.) Her second, more ambitious book – superbly adapted for television – was considered the most shocking of the Bells' novels when it was first published – (one paper described it as 'revolting' and made a special effort to warn off lady readers). Dealing with a young woman's attempt to escape with her son from a nightmarish marriage, its explicit portrayal of domestic violence, drunkenness, swearing and child corruption are utterly uncompromising, as is its message about society's need to question the macho values of so-called 'manliness'.

The Brontës' novels have long had to compete for attention with the romantic story of their life in Haworth which has, as Henry James put it, been made to hang before us as insistently as the vividest page of *Jane Eyre* or *Wuthering Heights.* Since the novelist Elizabeth Gaskell published her famous *Life of Charlotte Brontë* in 1857, only two years after its subject's death, Brontë biography has established itself as a genre in its own right. Hardly a year has gone by without yet another variation on the theme appearing, ranging from short potted versions to longer, in-depth accounts. The cumulative effect of this endless re-telling has been to shift the Brontë story from the level of history to that of myth. As a result, the family has come to occupy a curious no-man's-land between reality and fantasy, caricatured as three weird sisters playing out their tragedy on top of a windswept moor with their mad drug-addict brother and deranged misanthropic father.

If this melodramatic image, ultimately derived from Mrs Gaskell, has had a tendency to overshadow the sisters' literary achievements, it is not surprising. Strangely enough, Mrs Gaskell's original intention in writing her *Life* was not to celebrate the Brontës' novels, but to distract attention from them. *Jane Eyre's* initial success in 1847 had been followed by a critical backlash in which the outspoken passion of all three sisters' works was castigated as 'coarse, immoral and unfeminine.' The novels had developed a reputation for being, at the very least 'naughty', and when it became known that Currer, Ellis and Acton Bell were in fact three young women critics were all the more outraged. As a personal friend of Charlotte, Mrs Gaskell made it her mission to save the Brontë reputation by exonerating the sisters for having written such dubious books. This she did by exaggerating the tragedy and isolation of their lives in an effort to secure readers' sympathy.

The Life of Charlotte Brontë should certainly be read – it is a virtuoso performance – but one should keep in mind first that it is an apologia and secondly that it is the work of a novelist who confessed that she found it hard to 'keep to the facts, a most difficult thing for a writer of fiction.' In her quest to portray her subject as a saintly tragic heroine, she suppressed crucial material, such as the fact that Charlotte had fallen in love with a married man, her French teacher in Brussels. But she also drew heavily on the conventions and stock characters of the nineteenth century novel in her efforts to mould the raw material of the Brontës' lives into an emotionally and aesthetically satisfying narrative. If you are interested to know where the Brontës' first biographer was coming from, Jenny Uglow's *Elizabeth Gaskell: A Habit of Stories* is well worth reading.

Many biographers have followed in the footsteps of Elizabeth Gaskell. In the past, her novelistic precedent has had the unfortunate effect of unleashing waves of romantic apocrypha, which have mainly clustered around Emily, the most mysterious of the sisters. One biographer in the 1930s notoriously mistook the words 'Love's Farewell', the title of a poem in manuscript, as 'Louis Parensell' and went on to construct a completely bogus love affair between Emily and the said Louis. Another argued, quite seriously, that Emily had been possessed by the devil, while various false claims have been made that Branwell was the true author of *Wuthering Heights*. Readers picking up biographies in second hand bookshops have been warned, though one can occasionally find some interesting stuff nevertheless. Muriel Spark's 1953 *Emily Brontë: Her Life* (re-issued in 1993 in *The Essence of the Brontës: A Compilation of Essays*) offers an intriguing perspective on Emily's relationship to the Romantic Poets and Winifred

Gèrin's biographies of each of the siblings are still worth reading.

Today however, we are lucky enough to be living in a real golden age for Brontë scholarship. Charlotte's letters – which reveal her to have been far livelier, funnier and more opinionated than the drooping heroine of Gaskell's *Life*, have only recently been collected into a truly accurate and complete 2 volume edition. Non-specialist readers might prefer Juliet Barker's *The Brontës: A Life in Letters*, which is exactly what it says – well-chosen extracts strung together into a narrative.

Juliet Barker is also the author of the monumental biography *The Brontës*, which is essential reading for anyone at all interested in the family and their works. A previous curator of the Brontë Parsonage Museum, Barker spent eleven years researching the book, which sets the factual record about as straight as it will ever get. Instead of the windswept romance of legend, she reveals that Haworth was in fact a busy industrial township with many working factories and appalling public hygiene. No longer the crazy misanthrope created by Mrs Gaskell, the Reverend Patrick Brontë is shown to have been a public figure of some importance, involved in local politics. Most sensationally, Branwell (who was falsely accused of child sex abuse by Daphne du Maurier in her biography *The Infernal World of Branwell Brontë*) is revealed as the father of an illegitimate child. In her laudable efforts at demystification, however, Barker underplays the extraordinariness of the sisters' talents. She believes that the Brontë men, in contrast, have had a raw deal at biographers' hands and been unfairly portrayed as villains. In her desire to do them justice she sometimes seems to forget that they do not really merit such in-depth research except in their relation to Charlotte, Emily and Anne. Neither father nor brother, nor

Charlotte's husband Arthur Nicholls ever contributed anything lasting to the canon of English literature, and Barker's championing of Branwell's writings is somewhat misguided.

Biographical fact, which can be established more or less for certain, is not the same as biographical truth, which requires a leap of the imagination and is never more than partial or provisional. One recent book which perhaps gets closer to a deeper truth is Lyndall Gordon's compelling *Charlotte Brontë: A Passionate Life*, which, while accurate, is less concerned with factual minutiae than with Charlotte's emotional and artistic development. It puts the novels centre stage and offers the best sort of literary criticism, vivid, focused and intellectually grounded without being abstrusely academic. Another biography of Charlotte well worth reading is Rebecca Fraser's, published in 1988, which is particularly interesting on Charlotte's relation to the 'woman question' of the 1840s and 1850s.

Emily is a far less tractable biographical subject than her sister. Since so little material survives in the form of letters or diaries, any life of the woman so rightly called 'the sphinx of English literature' is bound to be speculative. Recent writers have kept their imaginations more firmly under control than many of their predecessors but their views are often still a matter of belief rather than knowledge. It is up to you to decide whether you prefer Katherine Frank's claim that Emily was anorexic (*Emily Brontë*, 1990) or Edward Chitham's idea that she was obsessed with Shelley (*A Life of Emily Brontë* ,1987) or Stevie Davies's suggestion that she had lesbian tendencies. Davies's view of Emily's sexuality is in fact the least convincing part of her *Emily Brontë: Heretic* which contains some fascinating ideas about the novelist's use of her intellectual heritage and some sensitive critiques of the few fragments of her personal writing which survive.

Anne Brontë has attracted far fewer biographers, but there are lives of her by Winifred Gerin and Edward Chitham.

Anyone wanting to read first-hand accounts of the Brontës by their contemporaries, rather than biographers' interpretations, might well be interested in *The Brontës: Interview and Recollections* edited by Harold Orel. But non-specialists are likely to get bogged down in Charlotte's voluminous juvenilia, which are disappointingly long-winded and boring. But Christine Alexander, who has edited this mass of material, has also published a critical account *The Early Writings of Charlotte Brontë* (1983) which is fascinating.

Finally, the Brontë Society regularly publishes its Transactions, offering eclectic collections of articles, ranging from short notes to deeper analyses, which reflect the latest scholarship.

Lucasta Miller is the author of The Brontë Myth. *Her book* Feminists and Cads *will be published in 2011.*

William Maxwell: writer of unmissable novels

Adèle Geras

About eighteen months ago, I read a review in *The Guardian*, written by Nicholas Lezard, which described a novel that was in many ways not of the twentieth century but of the nineteenth. The piece was so enthusiastic that I made up my mind to go in search of the book. I liked the sound of it. It was a family story, Lezard said, set in the Mid West of the United States in 1912. Its name was *Time Will Darken It,* which sounded wonderfully enigmatic and mysterious. I could hardly wait to read it.

When I saw it in the shop I liked the look of it at once. There are those who are attracted to covers sporting buxom young women in shawls; others hanker after futuristic gizmos of some kind, preferably in lurid colours. I'm drawn to pictures of houses. I'm immediately curious to know what is going on behind the doors and in the rooms hinted at by dark windows. There was a most beautiful house on the cover of *Time Will Darken It.* I bought the book and brought it home. Ordinary life was a little difficult while I was reading it because I became totally caught up in the narrative. I was absorbed in a way that adults seldom are because they do not normally have the leisure to give themselves up completely to someone else's world, in the way that children do when they enjoy a story.

Now the novel has turned me into something of an Ancient Mariner. I, too, stop practically everyone and metaphorically grab them by the lapel and in their ear I whisper: 'Read this book. Then read everything else this man has written, because he is a better writer than almost everyone else.' His name is William Maxwell.

I discovered from the blurb that he was born in 1908. For forty years he was an editor at *The New Yorker* and worked with Welty, Updike, Cheever, and John O'Hara.

His novella, *So Long, See You Tomorrow* won an American Book Award in 1980. He has written six novels and several collections of short stories. His novel *The Folded Leaf* (*Leaf* from now on, for reasons of brevity) was published in 1945, and *Time Will Darken It* (which I'll call *Time*) in 1948. I cannot imagine why it has taken so long for his work to reach us in this country, but I am grateful to Harvill for unpacking this treasure for us. I hope that they follow with everything else he has ever written.

When Maxwell was ten years old his mother died of Spanish 'flu. She had just given birth to his brother. The absent mother figures in much of his work, and colours his prose with a poignancy that is touching without ever becoming sentimental. Perhaps because of this loss, he is intensely interested in women, their feelings and how they think, but also their clothes and manners and intricate networks of friendship and rivalry.

When I try to describe what's so good about his work face to face, I just wave my arms about and repeat over and over again, 'You'll love this novel... go on, buy it... it's ace... it's just your kind of thing'. For the readers of *Books and Company*, however, I shall have to be a little more rigorous. Here then, are ten reasons to admire William Maxwell.

1) He is the model of a narrator who is both omniscient and unobtrusive. His authorial voice tells us everything in measured terms, calmly and with great intelligence so that when emotions are heightened, the language becomes poetic and it's easy to be moved to tears. His prose is spare, elegant, and uncluttered. Carroll's Alice wisely asked 'What is the use of a book without pictures or conversation?' She would have loved Maxwell, who is equally good at descriptions and dialogue.

2) He is interested in people. You might think that this was not such a very unusual attribute in a novelist but at a time when ideas, jokes, concepts, tricks, and puzzles predominate in a lot of fiction, it's wonderfully refreshing to find a writer who is NOSEY on our behalf. He tells us everything we want to know about the characters, going into the depths of their inner as well as their outer life. I think it's about time we admitted that part of the pleasure of reading novels is the desire to know everything we possibly can about all kinds of other lives and other people in particular.

3) Following on from the last point, Maxwell is not afraid of DETAIL. Max Ophuls, the film director, once said that it was the right details that made art and Maxwell has a sharp eye for furnishings, clothes, jewels, pictures and landscapes, which he manages to put in front of us with the utmost economy. For instance:

"The woman who entered the room a moment later was so small, so slight, her dress so elaborately embroidered and beaded, her hair so intricately held in place by pins and rhinestone-studded combs that she seemed, though alive, to be hardly flesh and blood, but more like a middle-aged fairy."

4) There is something strange and wonderful about his storytelling technique. It's not as straightforward as it appears. It's true that what he is principally concerned with are the relationships between people. In *Time* the main story (there are several very interesting subsidiary strands of narrative which deal with the children, servants, neighbours, colleagues, etc. of our hero, Austin King) describes what happens when relations from the South come for a visit. Their arrival is like a stone thrown into a pond... all sorts of waves appear on the surface of Austin's life, which I don't propose to give away here. The time sequence is linear. The point of view changes but even though we sometimes see what is happening through the eyes of Austin's young child, Ab, or the formidable Miss Ewing who works in his law office, we are always aware that Maxwell is there behind them, organizing and orchestrating the telling of the tale. And he has a quirk which lifts the prose into the realm of the extraordinary and also brings it very firmly into the Modernist tradition. It's this. Right in the middle of the most dramatic events, he stops telling us the story and puts in a meditation or a series of thoughts on a certain subject. In *Time* he suddenly has a list (that takes up a page and a half) of the things that you will find pasted into every family scrapbook. Such items as:

"two families seated along the steps of a band pavilion"
or
"the children wading with their clothes pulled up to their thighs"
or
"girls with young men they did not marry"
or
"a path shovelled through deep snow."

Check your own photographs against Maxwell's, and there's an eerie accuracy about it as well as a kind of poetry that springs from repetition in what is a sort of litany.

In *Leaf*, which is about the love between two young men and the chequered course of their intense relationship, suddenly in Chapter 18 we have a dazzling essay on the subject of journeys, which is relevant to the story even though it seems not to be. It's full of gems like this:

"He [your neighbour in the next seat on the train, say] will spread out his life before you, on his knees. And afterward... he will ask to see your life and you will show it to him."

5) He knows the secrets hidden in the hearts of his characters and is not afraid of strong emotions. At a time when the ironic, the sharp, the funny, the post-modern are admired, it's a relief to be able sometimes to listen to a writer who reveals and lays before us a character's most personal feelings, even when these might be considered insignificant. Petty jealousies that people don't even like admitting to themselves; unworthy thoughts, envy, secret resentments and the way we cover them up – Maxwell goes into these in detail, without ever becoming boring.

6) He is in no hurry. The leisurely pace of his writing (by which I don't mean plodding and pedestrian) assumes you have as much time to listen to his story as he has to tell it, which is all the time in the world. This is amazingly pleasurable. It's only when you read prose like this that you understand how much of what is produced today proceeds at breakneck speed, fizzing and bouncing and glittering along in a desperate attempt to be as instantly gratifying as television or the movies. Maxwell, of course, was writing in

pre-television days when his audience was not subjected to millions of visual images from morning till night. He evidently saw it as part of a writer's duty to bring a scene alive for the reader. Hallelujah!

7) He is concerned with structure. His books have a shape. Not just a beginning, a middle and an end but architecture within the story. Again, it's only by contrast with a lot of novels which spill out on to their pages willy-nilly in a kind of haphazard stream that we can see what a really well-put-together book is like. Seasons change, naturally, but within the passage of time there is a choreography of the narrative and the way it moves between points of view, from interiors to exteriors, from one house to another in the same street, say, that shows that Maxwell is a very careful composer of his text. Indeed the wonderful quotation which stands as an epigraph for the whole of *Time* comes from the seventeenth century painter, Francisco Pacheco and invites us to compare the novel with a painting: a landscape with figures. It's too long to reproduce here, but these extracts should be enough to show the flavour:

'It [the pigment] must not be dark; on the contrary, it must be rather on the light side because time will darken it…

As you get nearer the foreground, the trees and houses shall be painted larger… In this part it is customary to use a practical method in putting in the details, mingling a few dry leaves among the green ones…

And it is very praiseworthy to make the grass on the ground look natural, for this section is nearest the observer.'

8) He creates characters who remain in your memory after the book has been closed – the very opposite of cardboard.

Leaf is a novel about a deep love between two young men and what happens to this love when a young woman comes into their lives. We have, you might think, seen this all before but Maxwell's story is not in any sense hackneyed. The two young heroes, Spud and Lymie, are beautifully rounded creations, the kind of rare fictional characters you know you would recognize if they were to walk into a room. The sexual relationship that exists between them on an almost subterranean level is only touched upon briefly but it colours the story and it is this feeling which leads to the tragic dénouement. Also, and this is important, Maxwell is one of those writers who seem as interested in his minor characters as in his main protagonists. The fabric of his novels is woven through with men and women who spring into real life, even if they only appear on very few pages.

9) The setting for most of his work is the Mid West of the United States of America. The small town, the farms, and (in *Leaf*) the University with its fraternity houses and arcane customs and eccentric teachers provides a backcloth for many more detailed and particular houses and rooms – Lymie's boarding house while he is at University, the office of Austin King in *Time*, the gymnasium in *Leaf* and many others. It's not the most enormous canvas in the world and it's the very opposite of metropolitan and smart, but we get to know it well and Maxwell communicates his own love of the territory. We feel at home there.
10) These novels are not plot-driven or filled with incident. While you are reading them, there will not be nights when you find yourself staying up late to find out what happened next. What is much more likely is that something you have read, some image, some conversation, some nuance of

thought or emotion will stay in your mind and haunt your dreams when you sleep. And when you wake up, you'll look at the world with new eyes.

So Long, See You Tomorrow is a novella. It was written thirty-two years after *Time* and is a sad story of jealousy, murder and high emotion in a country setting. The brevity of the work and the simple style add weight to a story which in other hands might have become melodramatic. It's fascinating to come to it after reading writers like Raymond Carver and E. Annie Proulx. I feel that Maxwell may well have been an important influence on them and on other modern American novelists and short story writers. Perhaps now that his work is available here he will show us in Britain some of the things that words – the right ones, in the right order – can still achieve.

Adèle Geras has, over the last 34 years, published more than 90 books for readers of all ages. Her latest novels are Dido, *for young adults, and* A Hidden Life. *She is married to Norman Geras and they have two daughters and three grandchildren. Since writing this article she's gone on to read William Maxwell's other novels which have not been a disappointment.*

Enjoying Scott

Eric Anderson

A few years ago, the British Council asked me to entertain a visitor from Peking. I assumed she wanted to talk about education and was prepared for one of those encounters which consist of questions about how many students you have and how many people teach them. Neither at Eton, where I then was, nor at Oxford, did I find it easy to explain systems which work rather well but are so different from the experience of people from other countries that the best that can be hoped for at the end of the day is amiable misunderstanding.

However, when my visitor arrived I found, to my delight, that she had sought me out because, like me, she loved Sir Walter Scott. Her introduction to him had occurred in traumatic circumstances. The Red Guard had taken over the Institute of Foreign Literature in which she worked, piled the library on to a pyre in the courtyard, rounded up the teachers and taken them off to new lives as peasants in the countryside. All that was left in the ransacked building were some dilapidated volumes of the Waverley Novels pushed into a cupboard as unfit for the open shelves. My friend concealed these in her padded trousers as she left for her years of exile in the country and read them in secret, risking death if discovered reading a foreign book.

Now she was engaged in writing the first Chinese biography of Scott.

My own introduction to him was less dramatic. As a schoolboy in Scott's native city I had passed the Scott Monument on Princes Street often enough (although I did not bother to climb it, I am sorry to say, until visiting friends had to be entertained in my student days). My school, however, always prescribed one Scott novel a year, along with one Shakespeare play, one novel by Dickens and large tracts of English poetry and we were encouraged to enter for the Edinburgh Sir Walter Scott Club's annual essay competition for a prize worth, I recall, £7. 10s. I quite liked *The Antiquary*, the novel for the year and I very much liked winning prizes. So I had a shot at it, did win, and found myself, no doubt as the Sir Walter Scott Club intended, hooked for life. There was no prize for reading Dickens and I quickly realised that beside Scott he was really pretty second-rate.

We lovers of Scott, once a majority of the reading public, are now few and far between. In his own day Scott was a roaring success, the first best-selling novelist. Throughout Victorian times collected editions poured from the press and were to be found in every house where books were read. Until the centenary of his death in 1932, his popularity remained assured and his place in the literature of the English-speaking world seemed unassailable. Today, however, although he has some well-known admirers, like Tony Blair and Douglas Hurd, he is among the least popular of novelists. The academic world runs courses on Victorian fiction without suggesting that students need to read Scott first, as Victorian novelists and reading public had all done and no Scott novel has been set at A-level for more than a quarter of a century.

Somehow, between the 1930s and the 1990s, The Great Unknown has become The Great Unread.

But not, my visitor assured me, in China. There two rival translations of *The Heart of Mid-Lothian* had appeared that year and other translations were on the way. What on earth, I asked her, attracted Chinese readers to novels written nearly two centuries ago by a westerner from a small country on the northern fringes of Europe?

'Chinese people are not so impatient as you,' she replied. "They have time to enjoy a good story, and Scott gives them good stories. Then, people like me who lived through what happened in our own country know that he completely understood the forces which divide a community against itself. And – if you don't mind that I say this," she added shyly, "we recognize in his Scottish peasants of the seventeenth and eighteenth century the Chinese peasant of today."

If that testimony to literature's ability to leap over time and place is even half-true, why is Scott so little regarded? I think it is more for what he does not offer than for what he does.

The problem is that he does not concern himself with that staple of the twentieth century novel, relationships between men and women in love. There are splendidly-drawn women characters in his novels. He is particularly good at the forceful, opinionated, practical wives of tradesmen and innkeepers, or housekeepers who rule their households. The language of passion comes naturally from the mouth of Effie Deans in *The Heart of Mid-Lothian* and he is completely at ease with other characters of what my Chinese friend would call the peasant class, like the flirtatious Jenny Dennison in *Old Mortality*. Meg Merrilies in *Guy Mannering* is an uncomfortably genuine gypsy and Jeannie Deans, who walks from

Edinburgh to London to plead with the Queen for her sister's life, is a brilliant, full-length portrait of a decent, ordinary, religious woman touched into greatness by loyalty to an errant sister of whose love affair she disapproves. There are fine mandarin women characters too, but they are fine in public rather than in private. Di Vernon, in *Rob Roy,* the tomboy sister of loutish Northumbrian squireens, keeps her end up with a sharp tongue and a forward manner. Queen Elizabeth in *Kenilworth* or Queen Anne in *The Heart of Mid-Lothian* are every bit as convincing as Scott's Cromwell or his Claverhouse.

When I wrote a BBC drama-documentary for the Scott bicentenary in 1971, I remember Magnus Magnusson, who was the producer, waving my script and saying: "It's splendid. Just what we wanted. But where's the sex? Where's the sadism?" For the second we wrote in part of a scene from *Old Mortality* in which a covenanter is tortured into confession and for the first we had Scott's daughter Anne float across the screen in a diaphanous (and almost certainly unhistorical) night-gown. The truth is that sex was not part of Scott's stock in trade. He is no prude (Effie Deans has an illegitimate baby) but he is too well-mannered to invite the reader to be a voyeur at its conception. That is to be expected when you remember that *The Heart of Mid-Lothian* was published in the same year as Bowdler's *Family Shakespeare.*

Nonetheless it is undeniably a weakness that Scott's heroes and heroines speak to each other like human beings only when they are angry, like Frank Orbaldistone in *Rob Roy,* or embarrassed, like Alan Fairford in *Redgauntlet.* It is a curious failing in a writer who had been a romantic and passionate young man. Perhaps the fact that he was forty-two when he wrote *Waverley* had something to do with it. Perhaps the psychological scars of his rejection as a young man by Williamina Belsches inhibited him. There is an extraordinary passage in his *Journal*, written after the death of his wife (to whom he had been happily married and entirely faithful), in which he confessed that the wound caused by that first "love in all its fervour" had never fully healed.

Be that as it may, he recognized his limitations. He could not do what Jane Austen did so well. "Read *Pride and Prejudice* for the third time at least," he recorded in his *Journal*. "That young lady had a talent for describing the involvements and feelings and characters of ordinary life which is to me the most wonderful I ever met with. The Big Bow-wow strain I can do myself like any now going but the exquisite touch which renders ordinary common-place things and characters interesting from the truth of the description and the sentiment is denied to me."

But there are other subjects open to a novelist and Scott has talents that still make him worth reading. Let me identify three of them. The first is his "Big Bow-wow strain". Great occasions bring out the best in him. His prose kindles when his story presents him with a battle or a tournament, a trial or a royal progress. He would like to have been a soldier himself, had not a lame leg made that impossible, and he knew the whole blood-stained history of Scotland backwards. In his historical novels he only rarely needed to consult a book. "I am complete master of the whole history of these strange times both of persecutors and persecuted," he told a friend when writing *Old Mortality*, and that was no exaggeration. He liked to say, in an allusion to *Twelfth Night*, that he had an advantage over the historical novelists who imitated him: "they may do their fooling with better grace but I do it more natural". In *Old Mortality*, the skirmish at

Drumclog and the Battle of Bothwell Bridge are masterly descriptions of the ebb and flow of battle. The terrain and the tactics are clearer to the reader than they could ever have been to the participants, and even if the blood, sweat, toil and tears are less in evidence than "the plumed troop and the great war" you are in the grip of a story-teller who makes you want to know what happened next. Scott loved the military details. If you want to know how a mediaeval tournament was organized you have only to read Chapter 13 of *Ivanhoe*.

He was a practising lawyer, a Clerk of the Court of Session in Edinburgh, and his imagination is always fired when his characters enter a court-room. There is an electric moment in what he may have visualized as his own court-room when Jeannie Deans refuses to tell the easy lie that would save her sister's life and spare her the epic journey on foot to London to plead for a royal pardon. In *Waverley*, there is a moving scene in the court at Carlisle when a merciful judge offers an illiterate clansman captured at Culloden the chance to plead for his life and finds himself confronted with loyalty stronger than death:

"I was only ganging to say, my lord," said Evan, in what he meant to be an insinuating manner, "that if your excellent Honour and the honourable court would let Vich Ian Vohr [his clan Chief] go free just this once, and let him gae back to France and no to trouble King George's government again, that ony six o' the very best of his clan will be willing to be justified in his stead; and if you'll just let me gae down to Glennaquoich, I'll fetch them up to ye mysell, to head or hang, and you may begin wi' me the very first man.

Notwithstanding the solemnity of the occasion, a sort of laugh was heard in the court at the extraordinary nature of the proposal. The judge checked this indecency, and Evan, looking sternly around, when the murmur abated, "If the Saxon gentlemen are laughing," he said, "because a poor man such as me thinks my life, or the life of six of my degree, is worth that of Vich Ian Vohr, it's like enough they may be very right; but if they laugh because they think I would not keep my word and come back to redeem him, I can tell them they ken neither the heart of a Hielandman, nor the honour of a gentleman.

There was no further inclination to laugh among the audience, and a dead silence ensued."

In *Old Mortality* the military tribunal meting out rough justice to those captured at Bothwell Brig brings the ploughman Cuddie Headrigg (who fought only because his batty old fanatical mother told him to) in front of the implacable General Dalyell:

"Were you at the battle of Bothwell Brigg?" was the first question which was thundered in his ears.

Cuddie meditated a denial, but had sense enough, upon reflection, to discover that the truth would be too strong for him; so he replied with true Caledonian indirectness of response, "I'll no say but it may be possible that I might hae been there."

"Answer directly, you knave, – yes, or no? You know you were there." "It's no for me to contradict your Lordship's Grace's honour," said Cuddie.

"Once more, sir, were you there? – Yes, or no?" said the Duke, impatiently.

"Dear sir," again replied Cuddie, "how can ane mind preceesely where they hae been a' the days o' their life?"

"Speak out, you scoundrel," said General Dalzell, "or I'll dash your teeth out with my dudgeon-haft! Do you think we can stand here all day to be turning and dodging with you, like greyhounds after a hare?"

"Aweel then," said Cuddie, "since naething else will please ye, write down that I cannot deny but I was there."

"Well, sir," said the Duke, "and do you think that the rising upon that occasion was rebellion, or not?"

"I'm no just free to gie my opinion, sir," said the cautious captive, "on what might cost my neck. but I doubt it will be very little better."

"Better than what?"

"Just than rebellion, as your honour ca's it," replied Cuddie.

"Well, sir, that's speaking to the purpose," replied his Grace. "And are you content to accept of the king's pardon for your guilt as a rebel, and to keep the Church, and pray for the king?"

"Blithely, sir," answered the unscrupulous Cuddie; "and drink his health into the bargain, when the ale's gude."

"Egad," said the duke, "this is a hearty cock. – What brought you into such a scrape, mine honest friend?"

"Just ill example, sir," replied the prisoner, "and a daft auld jaud of a mither, wi' reverence to your Grace's honour."

The Scottish peasant (answering as indirectly, one presumes, as a Chinese peasant) brings us to the second good reason for reading Scott – the positively Shakespearean range of his characters. In real life he was completely at home with all sorts and conditions of men. As a young man he tramped the remotest parts of the border country in search of ballads and charmed men and women of all ages into singing them to him. In maturer years, he was equally at ease cutting trees at Abbotsford with his man of all work Tom Purdie or dining in Edinburgh or London with Wellington or George IV. If anyone ever "walked with kings nor lost the common touch" it was Scott. All sorts and conditions of men – and women – people his novels in a profusion rivalled only by Shakespeare and Dickens (although Dickens's social range is narrower). Scott's captains and his kings are not, in the fashion of today, shown with feet of clay, but as their own age saw them and they speak accordingly. Here, for instance, is Claverhouse, "Bonnie Dundee", on what drives him on.

"You would hardly believe," said Claverhouse, in reply, "that, in the beginning of my military career, I had as much aversion to seeing blood spilt as ever man felt, – it seemed to me to be wrung from my own heart; and yet, if you trust one of those Whig fellows, he will tell you I drink a warm cup of it every morning before I breakfast. But in truth, Mr. Morton, why should we care so much for death, light upon us or around us whenever it may? Men die daily – not a bell tolls the hour but it is the death-note of some one or other; and why hesitate to shorten the span of others, or take over-anxious care to prolong our own? It is all a lottery... It is not the expiring pang that is worth thinking of in an event that must happen one day, and may befall us on any given moment, – it is the memory which the soldier leaves behind him, like the long train of light that follows the sunken sun, – that is all which is worth caring for, which distinguishes the death of the brave or the ignoble. When I think of death, Mr. Morton, as a thing worth thinking of, it is in the hope of pressing one day some well-fought and hard-won field of battle, and dying with the shout of victory in my ear: that would be worth dying for, – and more, it would be worth having lived for!"

Scott is better though with my friend's Scottish peasants,

in other words with Cuddie Headrigg, or the fisherman Mucklebackit, with Mrs Howden or Meg Dodds, with Nanty Ewart or the grumbling gardener, Andrew Fairservice. He is equally good with people of the middle sort, pedantic enthusiasts like the Baron of Bradwardine or the Antiquary, and men of affairs like the Edinburgh lawyer, Saunders Fairford, or the Glasgow councillor, Bailie Nicol Jarvie.

Here, for instance, is Fairservice, whose response to the greeting, "Fine day," is:

"It's no' thar muckle to be complained o'"

and whose verdict on the Northumbrian fox-hunters who employ him is that they ride

"haill days after a bit beast that winna weigh sax punds when they hae catched it."

He is not a caricature, though, not totally predictable. The suggestion that he should move since he finds so much fault with where he is elicits this unexpected response:

"And to speak truth, I hae been flitting every term these four-and-twenty years; but when the time comes, there's aye something to saw that I would like to see sawn, or something to maw that I would like to see mawn, or something to ripe that I would like to see ripen, – and sae I e'en daiker on wi' the family frae year's end to year's end."

It is Fairservice's grumbles about the Union between England and Scotland that later bring this characteristically practical reply from the bustling Glasgow businessman, Nicol Jarvie:

"Whisht, sir! whisht! it's ill-scraped tongues like yours that make mischief atween neighbourhoods and nations. There's naething sae gude on this side o' time but it might hae been better, and that may be said o' the Union. Nane were keener against it than the Glasgow folk, wi' their rabblings and their risings and their mobs, as they ca' them nowadays. But it's an ill wind blaws naebody gude. Let ilka ane roose the ford as they find it. I say, Let Glasgow flourish! whilk is judiciously and elegantly putten round the town's arms, by way of by-word. Now, since Saint Mungo catched herrings in the Clyde, what was ever like to gar us flourish like the sugar and tobacco trade? Will onybody tell me that, and grumble at the treaty that opened us a road west-awa' yonder?"

That same argument is being played out in Scotland now – and in Britain too, as we contemplate closer union with Europe. Scott sets his novels in the past, but again and again brings you up short by the modernity and the sanity of his views.

It is that sanity, that broad-mindedness, that sense of being in the company of a man who saw life steadily and saw it whole, that is the third reason why Scott is rewarding to read. He suffered, in the twentieth century, from having invented the historical novel, for (with *War and Peace* conveniently forgotten) no-one cared for historical novels until the new vogue for them in the past decade. Scott is much more than a historical novelist. His novels are historical in the narrow sense of being set in the past and in the wider sense that they illuminate the forces which shape great events. Their interest, however, does not depend on battles long ago. Nor does it depend on historical figures, excellent as some of them are. They play only supporting roles in the action.

In reality, the novels appeal to the reader on two levels. They tell a good story, set in an authentic historical period filled with real people, but at the same time they explore the notions of progress, of civilized values and of those qualities which are the same yesterday, today and tomorrow.

A typical Scott novel is set in the midst of a conflict

between two ways of life – between Normans and Saxons, Cavaliers and Round-heads, Jacobites and Hanoverians, Royalists and Covenanters, or just between romantics and realists. Invariably the final answer lies somewhere between the extremes. The more attractive characters often yearn for a vanishing past, for Highland loyalties or for romantic notions of honour and chivalry, and Scott (historian, romantic and collector of antiquities) yearns with them. The more hard-headed realists look towards a future in which Scott actually lived and enjoyed living, a world of order and civil peace, of the counting-house and the court of law. Scott loves the excitement of past times but he views them (as, for instance, at the end of the tournament in *Ivanhoe*) from the Edinburgh of the Scottish enlightenment:

> "Thus ended the memorable field of Ashby-de-la-Zouche, one of the most gallantly contested tournaments of that age, for although only four knights, including one who was smothered by the heat of his armour, had died upon the field, yet upwards of thirty were desperately wounded, four or five of whom never recovered. Several more were disabled for life and those who escaped best carried the marks of the conflict to the grave with them. Hence it is always mentioned in the old records, as the Gentle and Joyous Passage of Arms of Ashby."

The ending of *Redgauntlet* typically effects a reconciliation between two attitudes to life, while leaving us in no doubt that the future lies with sense rather than sensibility. Redgauntlet, a grim Jacobite of the previous generation, has bullied a dispirited band of drawing-room Jacobites into a meeting at a remote inn on the Solway Firth to plot a third (quite unhistorical) Jacobite rising. To their horror he produces for them the elderly Pretender himself, ready to set himself at their head. At this moment General Campbell, commander of government troops, who had notice of this seditious assembly, walks into the room alone. For the conspirators and the Pretender, the expectations are arrest, trial and execution. Instead Campbell invites them to disperse. He wants "to make no arrests, nay, to make no further enquiries of any kind." His hearers are dumb-founded.

"Is this real?" said Redgauntlet. "Can you mean this? – Am I – are all, are any of these gentlemen at liberty, without interruption, to embark in yonder brig, which, I see, is now again approaching the shore?"

"You, sir – all – any of the gentlemen present," said the General, – "all whom the vessel can contain, are at liberty to embark uninterrupted by me; but I advise none to go off who have not powerful reasons, unconnected with the present meeting, for this will be remembered against no one."

"Then, gentlemen," said Redgauntlet, clasping his hands together as the words burst from him, "the cause is lost for ever!"

The modern world has won – but it has adopted as its own the generous, honourable dealing on which its opponents prided themselves. Victory, in Scott, always goes to the world of order but it is a victory softened and enriched by traditional virtues.

Where does a new reader begin? People say Scott is difficult to read. Some of his characters speak in dialect, but so do some of Dickens's and some of Hardy's. If you can manage the quotations in this article you can cope. He is admittedly lengthy, but you can skip. "I care not who knows it, I write for general amusement," Scott said; he wrote at the gallop and he expected to be read that way. When a correspondent complained that the fourth volume of *The Heart of Mid-Lothian* was not as good as the rest (a sound judgement incidentally) Scott merely commented that an author should be well pleased if three-quarters of his work found favour with the public.

Scott has suffered from the daunting dust-covered collected editions. You should pick out the best and ignore the others. Scott is at his best when his foot is on his native heath, and the early reviewers were right to commend the "Scotch Novels". The best of these are *Waverley, The Antiquary, Rob Roy, Old Mortality, The Heart of Mid-Lothian* and *Redgauntlet* – although other Scott-readers would want to include *Guy Mannering, The Bride of Lammermoor* and *The Fair Maid of Perth*. The best-regarded of the novels set in England are probably *Kenilworth, Woodstock* and *Ivanhoe*.

To test whether Scott is to your taste or not, I suggest you read chapters 2 to 7 of *The Heart of Mid-Lothian* (the first can be omitted), the second chapter of *Old Mortality* (but not on any account the first, which must be omitted) and the first six chapters of *Rob Roy*. If none of these appeals to you, the more domestic *Redgauntlet* or *The Antiquary* may be worth a try.

A new scholarly edition of all the novels has just appeared, based on the earliest editions. It reads more dashingly than the cumbrous collected editions, and Penguin have brought out three volumes from the series: *Kenilworth, The Antiquary* and *Old Mortality*. If it were not improper to advertise a book in which I had a hand, I would have added that Scott's *Journal*, too, is available as a paperback from the Canongate Press. There have always been people who found Scott the man more attractive than Scott the novelist; so that is another way to approach him. As John Buchan said,

"The greatest figure he ever drew is in the Journal, and it is the man Walter Scott."

Sir Eric Anderson, formerly Headmaster and Provost of Eton, Rector of Lincoln College Oxford and chairman of the Heritage Lottery Fund, has been a lifelong enthusiast for his fellow-countryman Sir Walter Scott. He has written and spoken about his life and works both in Britain and America, and his Journal of Sir Walter Scott *is the standard edition of Scott's diaries. Recently retired, he is currently writing, with Adam Nicolson, a book on Eton, and on his own a short book on Scott – for whom, he believes, a revival in popularity is overdue.*

Left Hand, Right Hand! revisited

Philip Ziegler

Osbert Sitwell was a writer of alarming versatility and prolific output. First he was a poet, and though towards the end of his life he reluctantly accepted that he would never be numbered among the immortals, it was in his poetry that he took the greatest pride. He wrote several volumes of short stories, two or three of which were outstanding of their kind. His novels were talented but crippled; he could invent convincing characters and present them against a background that was vividly described, but once he had got them there he had no idea what to do with them. Usually they just stood around and talked. He was in the first rank of travel writers – few were better at conveying the atmosphere of a place and making readers feel that they were sharing the author's experiences and enjoying the same delights. As a journalist he was accomplished and ingenious. His literary and artistic criticism was perhaps superficial but it was always zestful and often perceptive.

Little of his enormous output is read today and no great injustice is done to the author by this neglect. Only when he came to write his memoirs could it be seen that all these millions of words had been no more than a training-ground for his crowning enterprise. The varying skills which he had acquired over the years came to fruition in the four volumes of autobiography (five, if one includes the final book of essays on writers or artists he had known) which were published under the collective title of *Left Hand, Right Hand!* In this work all his weaknesses were translated into strengths. His memoirs made sense of his life. For forty years, Osbert Sitwell's pride in his aristocratic ancestry had co-existed uneasily with his conviction that the artist was the sole truly superior being. Only in his autobiography, where his background and upbringing were triumphantly transmuted into art, did these two ill-suited elements achieve complete reconciliation.

Osbert conceived the idea of his autobiography early in the 1940s and almost at once settled down to piece together the materials for the first volumes. Isolated in his Derbyshire home of Renishaw as he was for the greater part of the Second World War, such labours provided an agreeable and not too demanding pastime. There was a timeless element about them. His intention was that the most memorable figure in the work should be the father who had dominated his life, against whom he had reacted, and who now was sequestered in Italy, moribund perhaps, but very far from dead. To draw his father's portrait, he hoped, would exorcise the spirit which still haunted him or at least be a pleasurable act of revenge.

To publish such a book in his father's lifetime, however, would invite accusations of tactlessness at least, probably of ingratitude and cruelty – let alone the fact that he intended to quote – or misquote – lavishly from Sir George's letters and thus might well run into difficulties of copyright. "I sincerely hope your father will die soon so that the world can have the pleasure I had by candlelight from your autobiography,' wrote John Piper in mid-1942, stating with some brutality the problem that perplexed Osbert. Osbert more than half hoped the same, but could not foresee when the way would thus be cleared for him to publish. In fact, his work benefited by this uncertainty. One of his faults as a writer was that he would rush impetuously into a first draft, subsequently tinker endlessly with the text, but never eliminate the basic flaws. With the autobiography he was forced to chew the intellectual cud, so that by the time he came to write, the material was digested and the overall pattern and proportions were clear in his mind.

Osbert planned a work that would be richly opinionated but reticent on all the more intimate features of his life. He would tell the reader plenty about his thoughts, would leave nobody in any doubt about his views on Picasso or Piero della Francesca, the rival merits of the XIth Hussars and the Grenadier Guards, but would leave his emotional life discreetly veiled. By the time the books appeared he had for more than twenty years shared his life with David Horner, the man whom he loved more ardently than any other human being he had known. Yet there was only one cursory reference to Horner in the text, no hint was given as to the author's homosexuality there was a fleeting reference to an early love affair but in such insubstantial detail as to leave the reader uncertain what, if anything, had happened.

Nor were there to be descriptions of 'hair-breadth scapes i' the imminent deadly breach'. Largely this was because there weren't any. Osbert's was, for the most part, a life devoid of adventures except the intellectual. When violent action did occur – as in his periods at the Western Front between December 1914 and May 1916 – he played it down. Nobody should turn to *Left Hand, Right Hand!* for a picture of a wartime soldier's life or an explanation of how Osbert survived the campaigns which cost the lives of so many of his contemporaries. This is a chronicle of what he saw and thought and wrote. An exception is the General Strike of 1926 – an episode in which Osbert convinced himself, if few others, that he played a role of some importance. The result is not happy. Osbert emerges as well-intentioned but self-important and largely ineffectual. "It is extraordinary that a man of his humour can write like that of Lord Wimborne and the general strike", remarked Evelyn Waugh.

When she reviewed the second volume of the sequence, *The Scarlet Tree,* in 1946, Elizabeth Bowen wrote: "It seems to me notable that in England we have, as compared to France, almost no great writers about Society – its historical and monumental aspects, its rich and authoritative consciousness, its shifting values. In this aspect alone the almost unique importance of Sir Osbert Sitwell cannot be over-rated. He anatomises not a single life but an age." The reference to France is significant. One writer was evoked more often than any other when critics sought parallels for Osbert's achievement, and he was Marcel Proust. Osbert was immensely gratified. He revered Proust and was proud to have been deemed to follow in his footsteps. The comparison flattered him but not ridiculously. The parallels were obvious. Both writers were absorbed by the social minutiae of their age, both indulged in long discursive sentences which apparently rambled inconsequentially but were in fact subject to the most rigorous control. Osbert's use of memory was more controlled – more contrived perhaps – than Proust's, but both writers were fascinated by the shadowy, evanescent relationship between recollection and reality. But there were patent differences too. Osbert's spectrum did not encompass passion, he could not for the life of him have evoked the horrors of jealousy and frustrated love depicted so terribly in

Albertine Desparue. But then Proust could not have handled the great comic set-pieces of Osbert's memoirs, above all the descriptions of the author's father, Sir George Sitwell, and his faithful henchman, Henry Moat.

That Osbert's portrait of his father was unfair is incontestable. To take only one point, he edited Sir George's letters so as to make their author seem more ridiculous with an ingenuity that was as adept as it was unscrupulous. But though he enhanced the truth, he rarely distorted it. Sir George really was a grotesque on the grandest possible scale, a man who pursued his hobby-horses with sublime indifference to the feelings of others, almost, indeed, without being aware of their existence. As a Member of Parliament he had consistently failed to recognize even his most prominent supporters in the constituency; he was perfectly capable of cutting his children dead at a range of a few feet if his mind was on other matters.

He was a mediaevalist of some renown and tended to assume not merely that things had been better done in the Middle Ages, but that things were still being done in the same way in the Twentieth Century. When Osbert was at the Western Front, his father advised him, in case of bombardment, to do what he had done when the German fleet shelled Scarborough – take shelter in the undercroft until the danger had passed. Even when he remembered the century in which he was living, his grasp of reality was tenuous. Once he told his sons that he proposed to give an Artists' Party, which he hoped they would attend. The list of intended guests was indeed imposing; the only pity was that all of them were dead.

His knowledge of gardens, Italian in particular, was scholarly and extensive, and he employed his learning to great effect in the embellishment of the gardens at Renishaw and his Tuscan palace of Montegufoni. When it came to advising others, however, he sometimes strayed into the impracticable. "The secret of success in garden-making," he wrote, "is that we should abandon the struggle to make nature beautiful round the house and should rather move the house to where nature is beautiful." He brimmed over with ideas; some sound, many fantastical. He invented a musical toothbrush and a small revolver for killing wasps and maintained that the handles of knives should always be made from condensed milk. "But what if the cat gets at them?" enquired his ever-skeptical servant, Henry Moat.

Moat, Sancho Panza to Sir George's Don Quixote, played the role of straight man in this comic duo. He displayed unshakeable common-sense and a range of knowledge as varied and arcane as anything to which even his employer could aspire. He alternately reviled and revered Sir George, left his service indignantly from time to time but always returned after a few weeks or months, protected him, criticized him, defended him stoutly against anyone outside the family. He was frequently maddened by Sir George's vagaries but relished his absurdities and derived enormous pleasure from the relationship. "I never feel lonely when I just think of my past life. The cinema is not in it" he once told Osbert's mother, Lady Ida.

Sir George, when it came to buying furniture or re-shaping gardens, was capable of the most outrageous extravagance but in other matters he was cheese-paring, even miserly. His relationship with his sons was poisoned by his sustained but wholly ineffectual efforts to instill in them habits of economy and restraint. His attitude was in part explained by the damage done to the family fortunes by the army of parasites who had exploited the then baronet in the mid-nineteenth century. As a result he looked upon any sort of social intercourse with suspicion if not hostility. "Such a mistake to have friends", he once remarked, apropos of nothing.

"I want my memories to be old-fashioned and extravagant – as they are," wrote Osbert. "I want this work to be full of detail, massed or individual... I want this to be gothic, complicated in surface and crowned with turrets and pinnacles." They were as much baroque as gothic, sometimes, indeed, rococo in their detail. Osbert tacked to and fro amongst his memories. His recollections of mounting guard at the Tower of London as a young Grenadier were followed by a helping of his father's eccentricities and a vivid portrait of Sir Edwin Lutyens, a horror-comic account of his sufferings in a cavalry barracks at Aldershot led to a marvellously evocative description of the Russian Ballet in its first performances in London. Perhaps the most entirely successful section of the whole work recaptures the atmosphere of London's high Bohemia in the years immediately before the First World War. *Great Morning*, Osbert called the volume and bliss was it in that dawn to be alive but to be young was very heaven. It helped to be rich, too. Osbert was not rich, but he behaved as if he was, technically a Guards officer but rejoicing in the limited demands which that career made on his time and energies, flitting gorgeously from Mayfair ball to Chelsea salon, from plays to ballets to private views, overwhelmed by the genius of Nijinsky, Debussy, Chaliapin, rejoicing in the more homespun skills of Sickert, Bernard Shaw, Augustus John. He was avid for new impressions, open to every influence except the safe and conventional and though at this period he wrote little about what he heard and saw, the material was stored away within him to emerge enriched thirty years later.

When Richard Aldington reviewed the first volume of the autobiography he concluded that "to those who have the requisite knowledge and predisposition, it will be irresistible." The judgement must have filled Osbert with dismay. Of course he wanted – and got – flattering reviews, but reviews alone would not fully satisfy him. He had enough of succés d'estime, he wrote. What he wanted now was a thumping best seller which would make him lots of money and be found in every household with even the slightest pretensions to literacy. Aldington's suggestion that he had written a recherché masterpiece that would be caviare to the general reinforced doubts that he already held himself. His fears soon proved illusory. His publishers, Macmillans, were from the first certain that they had a success on their hands. They published a generous 20,000 copies and were confident that this would not prove to be enough. Even before publication they were reprinting. By the time the second volume in the series appeared the first had already sold 140,000 copies. The second did even better, the corresponding figure was 170,000. The edition produced by the Reprint Society was one of the most successful in the history of that institution. Traditionally the English bookshelf, like desert islands, was assumed to contain the Bible and Shakespeare. More recently the novels of Evelyn Waugh and the histories of Arthur Bryant had attained the same sort of ubiquity. Now *Left Hand, Right Hand!* took its place beside them.

Was such phenomenal success, critical as well as commercial, fully justified? When I was considering writing the biography of Osbert Sitwell, one of the first things that I did was to return to the autobiography. I remembered that I had read it with great pleasure when it first appeared, but would it have stood the test of time? I feared that I might now think it mandarin, long-winded, intolerably snobbish. To my relief I found that it was as fresh, as original, as funny, as when I had first read it. Certainly there are longeurs, moments at which one itches to be able to tell the author to get on with it, but they are not many and where they occur they are like the longeurs in *Parsifal*, excusable because of what they are building up to. Anyone who has never read or has forgotten them, who wants to know more about the period they describe, who is intrigued by human eccentricity, or who just enjoys good writing and good stories, should hasten to procure and read them.

Philip Ziegler is one of Britain's most distinguished biographers and historians. His works include biographies of Diana Cooper, Lord Melbourne (both to be reissued in Faber Finds), Mountbatten, Harold Wilson and Osbert Sitwell. His authorised biography of Edward Heath was published in 2010.

Re-reading *David Copperfield*

William Trevor

The familiar can be a marvel. The night train's arrival in the early morning, the taxi journey across the city from the Stazione di Santa Maria Novella, over the Arno by this bridge or that, into the narrow Borgo San Jacopo, the streets, the buildings, the tarpaulins being lifted from the newspaper stalls, the bells of Santo Spirito – nothing has changed. They've altered the reception area in the Hotel Lungarno, they've had a wall or two down, but the faces behind the desk are the faces of the last time and the time before. Across the Ponte Santa Trinità – the Neri di Bicci Annunciation on the way – coffee in the Giocoso is the same good cappuccino. The tall man from the bank comes in on time for his. The grey-haired waiter greets the lady with the limp.

Perhaps the pleasure of such re-visiting is a personal thing. In an age when people can go almost anywhere, can ring the changes for a lifetime, never once returning, it may be that novelty is the natural attraction, new boundaries broken for the sake of it, the world made small. It is perhaps imagination on my part that time has added something of its own to what I saw when first my fifty-lire coin lit up the Neri Annunciation or to what I heard when first I listened to Bach's Brandenburg Concertos. It is perhaps imagination that riches have accumulated in *The Good Soldier* or *A Dance to the Music of*

Time. Do I hold some record, I wonder, for my biannual return to *The Diary of a Nobody*? Like an addict intent on his fix, I reach out for *The Heart is a Lonely Hunter* and *A Handful of Dust*. Imagination or not, there is never disappointment.

At the moment I'm on page 757 of *David Copperfield*: Betsey Trotwood's confession that she is not widowed. "Betsey Trotwood don't look a likely subject for the tender passion... but the time was, Trot, when she believed in that man most entirely." Time was when David believed in his school friend most entirely. Time was when Mr Wickfield was happy, when humility was enough for Uriah Heep. But fate changes fortunes, retracts its own promises, punishes for the dismissal of its warnings, and yet is fickle enough to be gentle also. Time was when such complexity was bewildering: I was too young when I first attempted to read Charles Dickens.

On the shelves of the bookcase on the landing, Horace Annesley Vachell was represented more than once, with Warwick Deeping and Philip Gibbs, John Dickson Carr and Dorothea Conyers, Hugh Walpole in his well-thumbed glory. *The Garden of Allah* was there as well and the adventures of Bulldog Drummond, *The Chronicles of the Imp*, *The Stars Look Down*. They were books picked up in job lots at country auctions, their pages sunburnt at the edges and giving off a pleasant papery smell, their fly-leaves inscribed with names and dates. Then Dickens arrived to fill the empty bottom shelf; a dozen elegant volumes, gold-lettering on blue, obtained by my father with Sweet Afton cigarette coupons. Jane Austen and the Brontës came in red. Nobody opened any of them.

It happened that my childhood was a peripatetic one – the bookcase took its place on landings all over County Cork, moved on to Tipperary and on again to Enniscorthy,

Maryborough and Galway. I tried the job lots, then *The Cloister and the Hearth*, left behind by some visitor to the house. Familiar already with the illustrations and the portrait of Charles Dickens above a flamboyant signature, I cautiously approached the very thin, tightly-packed pages. On a summer afternoon in 1940 – the day old Canon Stringer, over tea in the warm June sunshine, passed on the gloomy news that France had fallen – I began *Nicholas Nickleby* in another part of the garden that stretched, long and narrow, behind our house in Tipperary, next to the gasworks.

No spell was cast. That rich, easy story seemed fussily complicated and with wearisome longueurs. The Phiz illustrations were a promise that was unfulfilled and remained so until adolescence took over childhood. *Bleak House* brought hope, *Martin Chuzzlewit* at least had Mr Pecksniff; and then, quite suddenly, what had been so teasingly elusive was less so. Some part of an tutored imagination responded to the vengeance of Miss Havisham behind her high gates, to her existence among stopped clocks and the mice that roamed the table of her wedding feast, responded to the beauty of Estella and a lawyer's whiff of mystery, to expectations denied.

When literature demands of its reader more than the experience of a child can bring to it, the surface is sometimes enough for the time being. Subtleties can be passed over, a kind of sense made of what remains, as the cinema so often quite successfully does with the fiction that attracts it. My introduction to *David Copperfield* was Freddie Bartholemew's interpretation of him, and it wasn't important in the least that Maureen O'Sullivan was gratingly miscast as Dora. Except for Edna May Oliver's the faces have all changed in the meantime, as Dickens has reclaimed what belongs to him. Only the toothy severity of that celluloid Betsey Trotwood, her flailing arms, stick raised to beat off the donkeys on her turf, is there for ever, and nothing is the worse for that.

After my slow beginning, Dickens impatiently took charge, carrying me away from quiet, provincial Ireland to the wild entanglement of London's streets, to the chill flatlands of Norfolk by the sea, to domestic Hertfordshire and marshy Kent, to the great drawing-rooms of the rich and important, to workhouses and taverns, to life that for me still throbbed almost a hundred years after he had recorded it.

My small-town experience could neither contradict nor confirm the detail of his pages. Nor did I wish it to. You trust the fiction you have come to love. I believed without an effort in Mr Dombey and Little Dorrit, in Major Bagstock, in Mrs Jellyby, in Mr Jorkins, until I realised I wasn't meant to. I accepted that graveyards' dead might still have a part to play, that ghosts would rise from beneath their tombstones if a quirk of the plot called them. Familiarity since has changed none of that.

Re-reading a novel sharpens into focus the blur of memory; grey paragraphs re-establish the detail of landscape and dress, the contents of rooms, the tone of voices. Encountering Peggoty and her family for the third or fourth time is to meet old friends again. And Mr Barkis seems more devious when the acquaintance is renewed, Miss Murdstone is crueller, Mrs Steerforth prouder. The kindness of Traddles, the wisdom of Mr Dick, the distress of the Micawbers, the self-pity of Mrs Gummidge. Noticed now are the variations on each theme that were noticed before. Miss Lavinia and Miss Clarissa are not different if their intentions are anticipated. The boyish husband and his child wife live out their mistake as movingly when they are shadowed by what is to be as they do when the outcome is not known. Rosa Dartle's bitterness still begs for mercy whether or not her wounded features are part of the plot. Great novels take it in their stride when their secrets aren't secrets any more.

The pleasure of re-reading *David Copperfield* now is not just for the story, its people, its twists and turns of human nature, but for the manner in which it is written. It is the manner that distinguishes all Dickens's novels, and the greater part of the fiction that has survived from the nineteenth century and before it. Dickens was not a notable stylist, but prose such as his, assisted in its flow by the grammar that exists for no other reason than to offer such assistance, is doubly a joy when the English language is increasingly polluted and vandalized. You are spared in *David Copperfield* – in *Our Mutual Friend*, in *The Old Curiosity Shop* or any of the others – the destructive rules of political correctness, indifference as to whether or not communication becomes muddle, the slapdash, the pretentious, the inept. That you escape so much is one part of the delight of re-reading well-written fiction. Another is that the story, now a reality in its own right, seems better than it did last time. As the Annunciation of Neri di Bicci does, or having coffee in the Giocoso.

William Trevor was born in County Cork and spent his childhood in provincial Ireland. He is one of the most distinguished contemporary novelists and short story writers and has won the Whitbread, Hawthornden and David Cohen Awards. He was knighted in 2002 and now lives in Devon.

The happy priest

Jane Gardam

Years ago, one wet summer in a chilling hotel on the North Yorkshire moors, my soul was saved by the Vicar of Danby, who had been dead for half a century.

We were having a week we could not really afford, a first holiday with our new and sleepless first child of six months, and we were not very popular because the bedroom walls were thin. The hotel had until recently been the house of a country gentleman but its inside had been gutted and changed. The antiseptic dining room was a place where one whispered, its exit guarded by two waitresses gaunt as vinegar bottles. The food was cheerless. There were notices everywhere about hours of availability of bathroom and the iniquity of doing washing. Where was the expansive Yorkshire I knew and loved?

The answer was, in the hall, stuffed behind a wad of magazines on the bottom shelf of a book-case which must have been the one thing the good squire had left behind him. It was the only book in the place and it was the right book, the perfect book: the Reverend J.C. Atkinson's *Forty Years in a Moorland Parish,* published by Macmillan, green cloth gold lettering, fine brown and cream map under tissue paper, charming etchings of moorland bridges and cruck-houses, first edition, second re-print, 1892, now I think 'very collectable'.

Atkinson was incumbent of the lonely parish of Danby from 1847 to 1900, dying in harness at eighty-six. He had many times turned down offers of higher office though the living was only worth £96 a year. He was a gentleman from an ancient family, son of an Essex parson and graduate of St John's Cambridge and never remotely well-off. Photographs show a worn and shiny cassock and he is said to have his leggings patched with the uppers of his old boots. His desk chair was re-seated with a plank. 'There is nobody rich here,' he said. The fine photograph by Sutcliffe of Whitby shows a happy man at a desk, an Old Testament prophet with books and the oldest typewriter in the world beside him.

Atkinson went to view his new parish as a young bachelor from Scarborough where he had been curate for three years. He went on horseback first to Whitby and then on the next day across the moors, over the country where the last wolf in England is said to have been killed. He saw an eagle and hen-harriers, buzzards, black grouse but no obvious road. He crossed 'wild and solitary tracks' and 'great ravines'. 'Danby?' someone had said, 'Why, Danby was not found when they sent Bonaparte to St Helena or they'd not have bothered'. 'Before me, looking westward was the moor. On either side was moor... Across the valley was moor again... Behind me was moor and nothing else but moor... and yet not dreary, nor could one feel altogether alone, for there... from the south east was the great wide open sea... and the sea, even at a distance is a creature – a being – full of great vitality and with many voices that aid... a most real communion with the unseen.'

He met a woman who pointed him in the wrong direction and then a huge cavalcade of oxen and horses drawing huge stone-wagons which made him wonder if he'd passed back into the Middle Ages. At Danby he found a broken, dirty church and a parson who kept his hat on and lit up a pipe as he showed him round it. He met poor moorland families where everyone, masters and servants, slept together in dormitories with disastrous results, sketchy morality and ludicrous belief in superstitions. He also heard a language he believed to 'pure Danish', people untouched by the agricultural and industrial revolutions, far, far behind, for example, the parish of Haworth to the west. He knew that the railways would come and he would have to work against time to record the dialect, folk-lore and wild life and the almost untouched archaeological history on the moors, and he took the job.

He first had a parsonage built, restored the church and set about working for better conditions for the farming people. He began the regular visitations to his flock with notebook and pencil. He estimated that in his first forty years at Danby he had walked seventy-thousand miles on parish duty and at least as many again for his 'recreation'. His 'recreation' was often a sort of mystical rapture and often hard digging into Anglo-Saxon barrows. He was blissfully happy. 'Angels would forget their wings,' he said.

While the Church was going through its Barchester phase Atkinson was classless, 'without side', liberal. He approved of dancing, respected other denominations, particularly the Quakers. He liked a pipe and a glass of wine. His prose was full of Latin tags and Old English but he was not an intellectual snob either. He would pounce on anybody to pass on a new discovery or new dialect word 'like an angler landing a fish'. He made his taciturn labourers on the moor jovial, took out 'two or three of my elder sons' – he had seven – to help him, organized great family diggings picnics. A passing stranger watching him uproariously at work enquired if he had 'found gow-uld'.

At Danby he wrote twenty-five books beginning with stories of moorland life, for children and going on to the ambitious *A Glossary of the Cleveland Dialect* (1868) and then his huge *History of Cleveland Ancient and Modern* (1872-7) which involved him in a lively lawsuit with a printer. In 1891 came *Forty Years* that brought him fame and was often reprinted by Macmillan. The Macmillans built a house near Danby – now Botton Village Community – and became great friends. Pilgrims and scholars began to turn up at the parsonage, sometimes welcome and sometimes not.

There is wonderful stuff in *Forty Years*. It is a little rambly now and then but without the pomposity or fruitiness of the times. Atkinson had a talent for phonetic speech and we can hear the authentic old Yorkshire voices. Many of the dialect words were to disappear in the coming generation and the stories fade out. Most of Atkinson's flock seem to have believed in fairies and hobs and demons and there is a horrible account of lads hunting a witch as dogs hunt hares.

He was not a great writer or a poet and doesn't seem to have kept a formal diary, though a huge amount of papers found in the roof of the parsonage after his death were destroyed. He was not a Kilvert or a great black brooding mind like Patrick Brontë. But he had better luck than either of them in his temperament and magnificent constitution, and a beautiful face. The parish called him 'honey' for years and 'bairn' till he was sixty.

And he had the advantage of Mrs Atkinson. In fact of three Mrs Atkinsons. A very good book, *Canon Atkinson and his Country*, by Tom Scott Burns (Rigg Publications £10) reveals all. The first was a genteel Scarborough girl whose photograph shows an unhappy face with downcast puffy eyes. She bore the Canon eight children and died. The second Mrs Atkinson appears mysteriously from Frome in Somerset, became mother of the next six children and died when her husband was seventy. He then married a rather unappealing-looking woman of thirty, called Helen, who enjoyed walking the moors. She outlived him, left Danby two months after the funeral for Canada and spent the rest of her life with reluctant relations. (They called her 'Old Hell') She died of fury in an Edinburgh boarding-house disputing a bill for coal. Yet Atkinson once said – and it's hard to forgive him – 'The first wife was good, the second one better but the third is the best of all.'

And what sort of a father? It is interesting that most of his thirteen children – one died – lost little time in putting the world's oceans between themselves and Danby and not one son became a parson which was very unusual in such families. One went to Canada and settled there, another was banished by his father for 'a misdemeanor'. One joined the merchant-navy and was drowned when he fell off his first ship. One became a GP and settled in the south. The last daughter, kept at home 'to help', escaped to London and married a very rich man with a title and never looked back. The eldest son, John, became a doctor and was the surgeon who went with Scott to the Antarctic.

Last year there was a great celebration in Danby to mark the centenary of the Canon's death. Five hundred turned up and relations from everywhere, most of whom had never met. The parsonage is exactly as he left it, the present vicar and his wife living there alone and marvelling that it had once housed seventeen people. The church, restored in Atkinson's memory at his death, is still the centre of the village. The vicar preached one of Atkinson's sermons for the occasion and it was pronounced 'very good'.

Atkinson's enthusiastic solitary scholarship of course has gone for ever, like the huge parsonage families, mobs of servants, spinster sisters and sisters-in-law who take charge when a wife dies; no cooks or governesses or Swiss laundry-maids for any money, let alone £95 a year. No subordinate, doomed, exhausted wives and no more vast, unhurried books of memoirs. And now, as Scott Burns says, the parish priests have to be overworked curateless parish organisers in cassock and walking boots marching to the lonely farms – though God knows such visits were never more needed. Anyway, I'm very grateful that, at a low ebb when I was the young, the Rev. Atkinson visited me.

Jane Gardam has won the Whitbread Award twice, for *The Queen of the Tambourines* and *The Hollow Land. God on the Rocks* was a runner-up for the Booker Prize. Old Filth is about the life and marriage of Edward Feathers, nickname 'Filth' – Failed in London Try Hong Kong. *The Man in the Wooden Hat* tells the story of his wife, Elisabeth, and how she became the reliable Betty of the first novel. Both stories are set against the end of the Raj. Jane Gardam was awarded an OBE in 2009. She lives in Yorkshire and in Kent and is married with three grown-up children.

Lilias Rider Haggard

Patricia Cleveland-Peck

The writer, Henry Rider Haggard is best remembered for his adventure tales. He wrote 58 books which gave rise to 30 films including *King Solomon's Mines* and *She*. In 1899 however, he compiled quite a different type of book, an agricultural survey of his Ditchingham estate, *The Farming Year*. Few people now know how important a subject the land was to Rider Haggard nor how he 'broke his heart and his purse on behalf of English Husbandry' as Massingham put it. Fewer still are aware that both this concern for the countryside and his literary talent was inherited by his daughter Lilias Rider Haggard. Lilias, described by an obituarist as 'a less inventive but a more graceful writer than her father,' published seven books of which her three country volumes *Norfolk Life, A Norfolk Notebook* and *A Country Scrapbook* are minor masterpieces.

She was born in 1892, the youngest of the Haggard's four children. The only son, Jock had died barely a year before, when only ten years old, a tragedy from which his father never really recovered. Any disappointment that Lilias was not a boy however, must have passed quickly for she turned out to be the quintessential tomboy, roaming the countryside throughout her childhood (she did not go to school until she was 14 and then only for a couple of years) acquiring a deep knowledge and love of natural lore. At quite a young age she became her father's constant companion, sharing with him his rural interests, as can be seen from a letter she wrote to him when he was away from home in 1912.

'My darling Dad,

...They have been ploughing steadily and several cows have calved. Willie Hood has I believe at last gone back to work. It's warm as possible down here and everything is growing like anything. ...

I have finished my thing on economy for cottagers and am trying to make Muriel practise it. I have almost persuaded her to keep a goat and now in the morning room and dining room we burn practically nothing but wood off the hill which I chop. I am becoming quite adept at it. It is put on damp to keep the fire in. Miss Turnbull sits and regards the fires with a mournful eye and casts longing glances towards the coal box. She remarked the other day she was thankful we did not have this craze in the cold weather as by now she would be a block of ice! As a matter of fact it is so warm one does not want much fire...'

Lilias was born and brought up at Ditchingham House, the home of her mother's family, the Margitsons. Here, as literary success swelled Rider Haggard's coffers, he acquired more land and made improvements to the house and gardens, projects in which Lilias collaborated with zest.

Lilias's youth ended suddenly with the advent of the First World War. She became a VAD and nursed the wounded, services for which she was later awarded the OBE. Photographs of her at the time show a lovely looking young girl and family intelligence has it that she may have fallen in love with one of her Australian convalescent patients. Whether this is true we shall probably never know but it is more likely than the other rumour in circulation – that she inspired the character Marion in L.P. Hartley's novel *The Go Between.*

In the summer of 1909 the young Hartley was a guest of a schoolfellow, Moxley, whose family had rented Bradenham Hall from Rider Haggard's brother. Many years later Hartley's sister claimed that her brother had found a diary there belonging to 'one of the young ladies' who had been taken abroad to get over an unsuitable love affair – and that it was this diary which gave Hartley the idea for the book. All quite possible, but improbable that Lilias was the young lady in question, as she would have been just 17 and although she visited Bradenham didn't live there.

Certainly, in her twenties Lilias did accompany her father on trips, firstly to South Africa and later when his health was poor, to Egypt. After his death in 1925 her mother relied heavily on her to run the estate, which consisted of 3 farms and numerous cottages. Lilias never married but was active in village affairs, served on the Parish Council and in every way lived the full life of a busy countrywoman.

Deep in her heart however, was a desire to write. She began by contributing a regular feature on country life to *The Eastern Daily Press.* She did not want to trade on her father's name so it was published anonymously. In fact, although Lilias appeared an extremely competent and definite person, the shadow of Rider Haggard's huge reputation probably sapped her self-confidence in literary matters for she even considered taking a 'writing-by-correspondence' course. Her own talent was vindicated however and her column quickly became one of the best-loved sections of the paper.

Emboldened by the success of this venture, she undertook

a most unusual task, that of editing *I Walked by Night.* As she says of the book 'What is written here was born of an old man's loneliness as he sat in a little cottage perched high on a hill, overlooking the Waveney Valley with no company but his dog.'

The old man was Rolfe, King of the Norfolk Poachers, who had written down his life story in penny exercise books. A farmer's wife who knew Lilias had 'a fancy for such things' passed these on to her, who in turn encouraged the old man to write more. She says in the preface, 'I have touched not on the story contained in these pages – the author tells it quite completely for himself' and having seen the original notebooks recently while on a visit to Norfolk, I can vouch for the truth of this – the impeccable copperplate calligraphy does nothing to prepare one for the author's inventive orthography and idiosyncratic style.

She followed this with a similar volume, *The Rabbit Skin Cap.* For this she edited the memoirs of George Baldry, a Norfolk countryman who had worked for her for many years. Both these books are entertaining and at the same time valuable social documents.

Meanwhile, in 1936 Henry Williamson had come to Norfolk with his family to embark on the project which he describes in his book *The Story of a Norfolk Farm.* At this very difficult time in his life Williamson derived such pleasure from Lilias' s anonymous articles that he asked the editor of the EDP who the author was. He then contacted Lilias and suggested that, well edited, these pieces would make a fine book and offered his services.

Lilias appreciated this as she was busy with estate business, so Williamson edited the text, added some footnotes of his own and then approached his publisher Faber who brought it out (bearing both names) as *Norfolk Life* in 1943. The book immediately went through nine printings and Williamson suggested to Lilias that they collaborate on a second volume. Lilias, however, had received a number of adverse comments on Williamson's contribution and although grateful for his assistance and above all for the introduction to Faber, decided to compile any further volumes on her own She tried to be diplomatic but eventually had to tell Williamson bluntly of her decision – after which, not surprisingly, relations between them cooled.

They did meet again for, coincidentally, Henry Williamson's first wife Loetitia came to live in the area after the couple's separation and she and Lilias became friends.

Now aged 97, and still living near Ditchingham, Loetitia Williamson remembers her well. 'A wonderful person. A great naturalist and a kind friend. When I came to live here (in 1949) the man I bought the house off told me Miss Lilias Haggard lived nearby – it was pure chance. My daughter had a pony and I didn't have any grazing so Lilias suggested that I let this house and rent her Wood House. It was Friday and I remember she gave me until Monday to make up my mind!'

Meanwhile Lilias had published *A Norfolk Notebook* and was working on *A Country Scrapbook*. Like *Norfolk Notes* these books have the immediacy of a diary while at the same time containing a wealth of folk-lore, natural history, quotations from the classics, asides on the books and of course, opinions on world events particularly relevant at this time, the run up to the Second World War.

'These are times which teach us the true value of our common surroundings...For what do men fight?...More often than not for one particular corner of their own country. For the memory of arable fields under a wind-swept sky; the fall of the valley to the river; the green stretch of pastures where they sweep up to meet the woods or the bare blue-misted hills. The place where they have been born or have been happy, or own some acres of earth.'

She plants potatoes, buys a cow, deals with evacuees and then evokes with simplicity and strength, the essence of the English countryside for which the soldiers were fighting.

'When I went out after supper to shut up the hens, two fields were cleared and the stack finished. The children had ridden back triumphantly on the last full sweep of hay, and had brought the horses up to the stack yard, while the men gathered forks and coats and came slowly after them down the hedgerow. Behind the oaks the sun was setting, leaving the long wind-blown wings of fiery cloud stretching upwards across the sky...and the dark shadows lying upon the fields grew blue and misty in the twilight.

After 12 years Lilias gave up her column in the EDP, claiming with her usual forthrightness that she was 'written out'. She did however, undertake several other projects, an affectionate biography of her father, *The Cloak that I Left,* published in 1951, a series of articles for the parish magazine which she wrote each month from 1961 and her last book, *Too Late for Tears,* which she says her father would have called 'small beer' as it does not claim to be more than a family chronicle, based on the diaries of a great-aunt. She died at Ditchingham House in 1968.

Patricia Cleveland Peck was a regular reader of and occasional contributor to Books and Company.

J.L. Carr's *A Month in the Country*

Penelope Fitzgerald

I first heard of J.L. Carr through a passage in Michael Holroyd's *Unreceived Opinions*. Holroyd had had from George Ellerbeck, a family butcher in Kettering, a letter telling him that he had won the Ellerbeck literary award, a non-transferable meat token for one pound of best steak and a copy of Carr's novel *The Harpole Report*, (so this must have been 1972 or 73). The letter went on, 'The Prize is only awarded at infrequent intervals and you are only its third recipient. The circumstances are that Mr Carr, who makes a living by writing, is one of my customers and pays me in part with unsold works known, I understand, as Remainders.' Never before or since have I heard of anyone who managed to settle up with a butcher, even in part, with Remainders. It is a rational and beneficial idea but it took Jim Carr to carry it out.

James Lloyd Carr was born on May 20th 1912 of a Yorkshire Methodist family. His father used to preach in the Wesleyan 'tin tabernacle.' Jim used occasionally to play truant but did not and could not forget the old Revivalist hymns – *Hold the Fort, Count your Many Blessings, Pull for the Shore, Sailor, We are Out on the Ocean, Sailing*. He went to the village school at Carlton Miniott in the North Riding and to Castleford Grammar School. At Castleford, his Headmaster was the enthusiastic and progressive 'Toddy' Dawes who, during a miners' strike, took the local brass band across to France to perform in Paris, where it won a competition. 'Other schools had ordinary Headmasters,' said Carr. 'We had Toddy.' In turn he himself became a teacher and a publisher of historical maps and delightful tiny booklets, *The Little Poets* – a little, that is, of each poet and illustrations of all sizes. These were left by the checkouts of bookshops to attract last-minute purchasers and on occasion, he gave them away, like sweets. I only wish I had a complete set now.

In 1977 he had reached pensionable age and retired. He settled not in his native Yorkshire but in Northamptonshire, where he had been a head teacher. He described it as 'onion fields, spud and beet fields, mile after mile of hedgeless flatness, dykes and ditches.' And he loved it dearly.

In 1979 he wrote his masterpiece, *A Month in the Country*, which was published in 1980, shortlisted for the Booker Prize and won the Guardian Fiction Prize. It was made into a film. 'Fine gentlemen from London,' as Jim insisted on calling them, arrived at his house in Kettering and pointed out that the title, of course, would not do, it had already been used by Turgenev. 'Is that so?' said Jim. 'I don't think I'll change mine though.' He didn't.

A Month in the Country is not quite like any other of his novels. It is 1920 and Tom Birkin is back from the trenches with a facial twitch which doctors tell him may get better in time. He has been trained by one of the last remaining experts as a restorer of medieval murals and he has been hired to uncover the whitewashed-over fourteenth century paintings on the wall of a Yorkshire village church. His fee will be twenty-five guineas and he is told to make the best of what he can find.

He arrives at Oxgodby station in pouring rain and

darkness but receives an offer to come inside and have a cup of tea from the stationmaster, Mr Ellerbeck. (The name of course, and the kindness, are from Kettering. Carr liked to introduce characters from one book into another and from real life into books.)

But Birkin refuses the offer. He has an appointment to meet the vicar at the church and in any case he is quite unused to northerners. He feels himself in an enemy country.

The rain stops and the next day brings the cloudless, golden, incomparable summer of 1920. For Tom Birkin, 'nerves shot to pieces, wife gone, dead broke,' it will be, almost against his will, a healing process. Like Solzhenitsyn in *Matryona's House,* he has wanted to cut himself off and lose himself in the innermost heart of the country. 'Only time would clean me up,' He thinks. But he is brought back to himself first of all by the way things are made. Even in the drenching rain he notices that the church masonry is 'beautifully cut, with only a hint of mortar.' Then there's the way things work, notably the cast-iron Bankdam-Crowther stove in the church itself. 'There seemed to be several knobs and toggles for which I could see no purpose. 'Plainly this damned big monster was going to provide me with several pleasurably instructive hours learning its foibles.' Then there is the place. On his very first morning in the bell tower a vast and magnificent landscape unfolds. 'Day after day, mist arose from the meadow as the sky lightened and hedges, barns and woods took shape until, at last the long curving back of the hills lifted away from the plain... day after day it was like that and each morning I leaned on the yard gate dragging at my first fag and (I'd like to think) marvelling at this splendid backcloth. But it can't have been so. I'm not the marvelling kind. Or was I then?' Next, there is the long-dead wall painter himself, 'a nameless painter, reaching from the dark to show me what he could do, saying to me as clear as any words, 'If any part of me survives from time's corruption, let it be this. For this is the sort of man I was.' (At the very end of the book, Birkin refers to him as 'the secret sharer,' a reminder that Carr had been given what he called his 'first stiff dose of Conrad' at Castleford Grammar School.) Lastly, as his unconscious healers, are the natives of Oxgodby, who turn out to be anything but hostile. Carr always dwelt lovingly not only on turns of speech but on details of behaviour that separate one region of England from another. He used to describe, for example, a down-and-out travelling show in Yorkshire, in which the compére had appealed for someone to come forward from the audience. But, said Jim, they don't 'come forward' in the North Riding.' Certainly they don't need to in Oxgodby, where they are used to speaking out and staying put. Kathy Ellerbeck, yelling her Mam's invitation to Sunday dinner up Birkin's ladder, is Carr's heartfelt tribute to the Yorkshire school-leaver.

The epigraphs of his books were important to him. *A Month in the Country* has three. The first is from Dr Johnson's *Dictionary*, a Carr-like, and indeed Johnson-like throwaway. The third was added to the 1991 edition after the death of Carr's wife, Sally. The second is from the poems he loved best, Housman's *A Shropshire Lad.* (No XXXII) I am here on earth only for a short time, Housman says. You must trust me.

Take my hand quick and tell me,
What have you in your heart?

Being Housman he is not likely to expect an answer and Birkin does not get one either.

There are, it turns out, three strangers in Oxgodby besides Birkin himself. One of them, Moon, he meets on his first day in the bell tower. We don't exactly know what Moon does, although he appears to be a professional archaeologist and had 'an RFC pal to fly him over the site before he began on his commission which is to make reasonable efforts, over a given period, to find a lost fourteenth-century grave. We do, however, find out, from a chance revelation in a Ripon tea-shop, the secret of Moon's war record, and what was done to him.

Birkin is working at the top of his ladder, Moon has dug himself a hole to live in beneath his bell-tent. Birkin has been accepted from the beginning by the inhabitants of Oxgodby, helps with the 'dafties' at the Wesleyan Sunday School, goes on the glorious Sunday School outing, to which Moon is not invited. Moon talks posh, Birkin doesn't, but he and Moon like each other. Are they to be thought of as opposites or as two marked men – marked that is by the war and their bitter experiences of sex and regarded by old Mossop the sexton as (like all southerners) fair caution?

The other two outsiders (or at least they haven't managed to feel accepted in Oxgodby) are the Vicar and his wife, Arthur and Alice Keach. (He is also referred to as the Rev. J.G. Keach, but Carr was a reckless proof-reader. He had, he said, a 'terrible and inexcusable vice of not reading a proof until after I have published it.')

The vicar is business-like –this seems at first to be his only good quality- disapproving, unyielding and chilly. He has 'a cold, cooped-up look about him,' and although he must have got used to the twitch, he continues to talk to someone behind Birkin's left shoulder. Cold church, warm chapel. Birkin listens through the floor of the belfry to the congregation 'bleating away; downstairs and contrasts it with the thick Yorkshire pudding at the Ellerbeck and the blacksmith's splendid basso-profundo. The vicar's wife, Alice, on the other hand, is like a Botticelli – the Primavera not the Venus – a Primavera, that is, with a straw hat with a rose from the vicarage garden stuck in the ribbon. Birkin's feelings for Alice are what might be expected and there is a moment when he is very close asking Housman's question, 'What have you in your heart?' His attitude to the vicar is also predictable. He and Moon have decided that the marriage is an outrage. 'Frankly, if Keach was as awful as he seemed, living with him didn't bear thinking about.'

But Birkin runs out of money and finds himself obliged to call round at the vicarage to ask for his first instalment of pay. This leads to a passage characteristic of Jim Carr, who likes to beguile us with a story based on his own experience or something near it, and then allow it to take off, just for a while, into a dazzling, improbable flight.

'The house was in a clearing, but what had once been a drive around for carriages was now blocked by a vast, stricken cedar, its torn roots heaving up like a cliffside and supporting a town sized garden, its crevices already colonised by wild plants.'

After a heroic struggle with the bell-pull, Birkin has the door opened to him by Alice Keach herself. She begins a not quite sane story about her life in the vicarage where the trees, it seems to her, are closing in on them until mercifully fended off at the last moment by the house walls. She has none of the self-assurance that she shows outside her home. The vicar too is different. He has evidently been playing his violin which is lying by a rickety music stand in one of the vast, chill rooms. Fig leaves like giant hands press against the window. The two of them seem huddled together for the comfort of each other's company. And Birkin feels unexpectedly sorry for the Reverend Arthur Keach.

It seems that the only people in the book we are asked thoroughly to disapprove of, even to hate, are the military authorities who sentenced Moon, and the grand new proprietor of The Baines Piano and Organ Warehouse in Ripon, who looks down on the Oxgodby deputation. (Mr Ellerbeck, his daughter Kathie, Mr Douthwaite the blacksmith and Birkin) who have come to replace the Wesleyans harmonium with a pipe organ. The proprietor thinks he can afford to despise them because they have come to buy second-hand, bringing the cash they have collected with them, in a bag. But he is greatly mistaken.

'It is the death of the spirit we must fear,' is Carr's epigraph, this time for his novel *The Harpole Report*. The death of the spirit is to lose confidence in one's own independence and to do only what we are expected to do. At the same time it is a mistake to expect anything specific from life. Life will not conform.

'And it's gone, it's gone, all the excitement and pride of that first job. Oxgodby, Kathie Ellerby, Alice Keach, Moon, that season of calm weather – gone as though they'd never been.' Early in the book the perspective of time is established. Birkin is looking back with wonder at the very last years of a lamp-lit, horse-drawn age. Of course he and Moon have another set of memories to haunt them, from Passchendaele. But Birkin believes that the future is opening up. 'Well I was young then.'

Carr is by no means a lavish writer, but he has the magic touch to re-enter the imagined past. Birkin notices as he walks back down the road, how he first smelled, then saw, the swathes of hay lying in the dust. At the Sunday School outing afterwards some of the men took off their jackets, exposing their braces and the tapes on their long woollen underwear and astonished the children by larking around 'like great lads.' Those tapes! Who would have remembered them except Jim Carr?

From the first Birkin has seen that the wall painting is a Doom, a Christ in Judgement, with its saved and its sinners in a great spread of reds and blues. He finishes the restoration according to contract just as the first breath of autumn comes to Oxgodby. But the moment when the year crosses into another season becomes indistinguishable from his passion, making itself clear as it does quite suddenly, for Alice Keach.

'All this happened so long ago.' The tone of *A Month in the Country*, however, is not one of straightforward remembering or, if there can be such a thing, of straightforward nostalgia or even an acute sense of the loss of youth. More complex is his state of mind when he thinks of the people – perhaps only a few – who will visit Oxgodby church in its meadows, and regret that they missed seeing the master painter himself – 'as one might come to Malvern, bland Malvern and think that Edward Elgar walked this way to give music lessons.' This is nostalgia for something we have never had, 'a precious tugging of the heart – knowing a precious moment gone and we not there.' But even this has to be distinguished from downright pain. 'We can ask and ask but we can't have again what once seemed ours forever.' You can only wait, Carr says, for the pain to pass, but what is it that once seemed ours forever? Or is this, like the Shropshire Lad's, an unanswerable question?

Rooms of their own

Margaret de Fonblanque

'It is necessary to have £500 a year and a room with a lock on the door if you are to write fiction or poetry,' said Virginia Woolf in 1928. Or indeed if you were to lead any kind of independent life free from the constraints of family or marriage. But what were they like, these rooms? And what sort of life did the independent women writers of the 1920s live in them?

Firstly, they were in the wrong place. Edith Sitwell lived in Bayswater, in Pembridge Mansions, a building designed in the 1870s for the respectable lower middle classes. It looked, said a friend, like an inexpensive and dirty hospital, 'hardly an address at which one would expect to find a Sitwell,' her biographer dryly observes. Edith herself explained to a visitor that Pembridge Mansions 'is the untidy, dingy, badly lighted block of flats just past the garage clock.' Her brothers Osbert and Sacheverell, more appropriately occupied an elegant little house in Chelsea. Ivy Compton Burnett was another Bayswater resident, living for years on the unfashionable north side of Hyde Park. Vera Brittain and Winifred Holtby shared rooms in Bloomsbury, handy for the British Museum but not fashionable, despite Virginia Woolf and certainly not fashionable in any way that would be appreciated by Mr and Mrs Brittain's friends and relations in Buxton. Dorothy L

Sayers and her fictional heroine Harriet Vane lived in Bloomsbury too. Lord Peter Wimsey did not. It was a question of cost and though many women writers came from comfortable professional backgrounds, money was an ever-present concern.

Money and perhaps convention and companionship meant that rooms were usually shared, Edith Sitwell with her former governess, Vera Brittain with a college friend, Ivy Compton Burnett with the formidable freelance writer and expert on interior design Margaret Jourdain. Dorothy Sayers lived on her own for many years, until her marriage, and so did Nancy Cunard in Paris. But neither led lives which would have met with approval in the Brittain's Buxton.

Decoration of the rooms depended upon interest as much as upon money. Edith Sitwell was intensely visually aware but poor. She rejected her father's offer of discarded curtains from Renishaw, the vast family house in Derbyshire but accepted some from her brother Osbert. As a result, her sitting room was hung with red and gold, her companion's with green and silver. 'All Edith's furniture is derelict,' said Virginia Woolf, 'to make up for which she is stuck about with jewels like a drowned mermaid.' There is a portrait of her in Pembridge Mansions in 1919 wearing a long green and gold robe, sitting upright in a cane chair in a room dominated by greens and red, with woven red and yellow rugs on the dark wooden floors and a large comfortable armchair smothered and green and red cushions behind her. It looks surprisingly cosy.

Margaret Jourdain, with a professional interest in furnishing, managed a style that was supremely unhomely. It was based on 'a few fine pieces of furniture arranged round walls distempered pale grey,' and hung with mirrors to emphasise space – and bareness. Miss Jourdain did not like ornaments and Miss Compton Burnett did not like flowers. There was lino instead of carpet, the plumbing was uncertain and the bedrooms were unheated.

Nancy Cunard was another writer with a sense of style but money was less of an issue for her and comfort rather more. She employed a maid to look after her flat on the Ile St Louis, with its view of Notre Dame. The sitting room had 'smokey red walls above black wainscoting, a plum coloured velvet sofa and walls hung with new paintings, including one of a man with 'four pairs of eyes, a body spotted all over with vermilion dots and one arm sheathed in black.' Nancy, an acquaintance of the Sitwells, shared their advanced tastes.

Vera Brittain and Winifred Holtby started off their careers in a studio flat carved out of 'one large high room lighted only by windows in the roof and divided by thin matchboard partitions into two tiny bedrooms, a minute sitting room and a kitchen so small that two of us and the gas cooker could not comfortably inhabit it at the same moment,' Vera wrote later. It was perhaps the freezing cold and the lack of sunlight that made Winifred's description of the flat shared by her heroines in *The Crowded Street* so heartfelt. There are blue curtains and hand-painted lampshades and 'the most luxurious of soft armchairs,' bowls of yellow roses and tawny chrysanthemums, firelight leaping on the plain blue carpet, a piano, books and a flower-decked table. So different from the studio in Doughty Street.

Dorothy Sayers gives Lord Peter Wimsey firelight, books and a grand piano in his flat in Piccadilly. He also has some fine prints on the wall, an Aubusson carpet, a vast Chesterfield and a number of deep and cosy armchairs upholstered in brown leather. As his creator cheerfully admitted, 'it gave me pleasure to spend his fortune for him. When I was dissatisfied with my single unfurnished room I took a luxurious flat for him in Piccadilly. When my cheap rug got a hole in it I ordered him an Aubusson carpet.' Harriet Vane was accorded no such comforts and Dorothy herself made the best of what she could afford. In 1920 she moved into a room in a Georgian house in Mecklenburg Square with three great windows she could not afford to curtain, a balcony overlooking the square, a coal fire (Lord Peter burned logs,) and no electricity. 'I shall get a little oil lamp,' she wrote to her parents, 'which will look very nice.' A year later she found three rooms nearby, a sitting room, bedroom and kitchen with use of a newly installed bathroom and lavatory. She reported to her parents that the rooms were quite small but very pretty, newly painted and panelled in white, which she felt would set off her pictures. She bought new curtains of a very loud colour and pattern that proved a success and a couple of Persian rugs that matched the curtains. The floor was stained dark and she had an armchair covered in black and gold, 'very good for not showing the dirt.'

Rosamund Lehmann does not give her heroine Olivia much choice about furnishings in *The Weather in the Streets*, since she shares her cousin Etty's house, but it is obviously not to her taste. There are references to the crammed 'doll's house sitting room... strangled with cherry coloured curtains, with parrot green and silver cushions, with Etty's little chairs, tables, stools, glasses and shagreen and cloisonné boxes, bowls, ornaments.' Miss Jourdain would not have approved. Nor, indeed, did Olivia.

Furnishings were a problem. Food was another. 'Food is my most sinful extravagance,' wrote Dorothy Sayers, though before Lord Peter made her rich she had little chance to indulge that particular sin. She enjoyed cooking, ('I do like cooking nice dinners,') and describes one meal to her mother with great pride. 'Grapefruit on ice with whipped cream, consommé, beefsteak with potatoes and salad, fruit jelly with cream, baked mushrooms,' and none of them came out of tins –' except the jelly mixture of course'– all accompanied by Vermouth, Spanish Burgundy, coffee and Grand Marnier. Virginia Woolf, who contrasted the delicious soles in cream sauce, the partridge and the wine at a lunch party at a men's college in Oxford with the prunes and custard provided for dinner at a women's college, would have sympathized with her enthusiasm. ('The water jug was liberally passed round,' she noted.)

It was an enthusiasm shared by Winifred Holtby. There are wistful references in *The Crowded Streets* to soup in a blue and yellow bowl and the fish soufflé produced by Muriel, who was clearly a good cook. In real life, Winifred and Vera were provided with a scanty breakfast on a tray by the blowsy, henna-haired housekeeper of the adjacent lodging-house, ate their lunch at a restaurant in Theobald's Road and made their own tea and supper in the tiny kitchen. But it is obvious that their priorities were crouching over the gas-fire in the sitting room working on their novels, speeches, teaching notes and what Vera describes poignantly as 'scores of permanently homeless articles.'

Edith Sitwell simply gave up the struggle. Guests were invited for tea or possibly for drinks. 'Dinner is impossible owing to the primitive nature of the cooking,' she wrote firmly. According to a friend, Edith and Helen lived off tea, bone broth and white beans and glazed penny buns. Despite the buns her tea parties were very well attended.

Rather surprisingly, given their disregard for comfort, Ivy Compton Burnett and Margaret Jourdain did believe in good food, 'roast meat or fowls, great joints of ham or bacon, steamed salmon with lavish helpings of parsley butter, following by nursery puddings such as junket, meringues and stone cream.' There was also a maid to help.

In stipulating £500 a year Virginia Woolf was perhaps pitching her demands rather high. It was certainly more than many women writers had to live on, at least before they achieved success. Edith Sitwell had £100 a year in 1914 and her companion rather less. They paid twenty-five shillings a week for three small and under-furnished rooms. Dorothy Sayers earned £4 a week in her advertising agency in 1923, later increased to £5 a week. 'If only one could make £250-£300 a year,' she pondered wistfully, 'one could live where one liked and go where one liked.' Winifred Holtby and Vera Brittain both taught in order to make money, though never full time. They were sorry for friends who had to resort to such desperate measures.

The subject of money permeates much of the private correspondence of the writers. None of them were likely to end up on the streets, literally or metaphorically. There was always a safety net. Sir George Sitwell's generosity was not to be relied upon – he had allowed his wife to go to prison rather than pay her debts himself, but Osbert and Sacheverell would undoubtedly have helped Edith as much as they could. Ivy Compton Burnett's father was a doctor, Dorothy Sayers's a clergyman. Sayers' parents were only too anxious to help out with gifts of cutlery or woollen underwear, (for which Dorothy was not grateful,) or in having her back at home in the fenland village where her father was Rector. Vera Brittain's parents had not wanted her to leave home in the first place.

This was, of course, the crux of the matter. To accept more than occasional help, above all to return home, was to admit failure and defeat. Vera Brittain wrote with relief of the penurious and unhumiliating independence of Bloomsbury, in contrast with her life of 'disappointing spinsterhood', as her parents saw it, at home. The loss of independence was something they were all determined to avoid. Compared with that £500 a year was a luxury. The essential thing was a room of one's own.

Margaret de Fonblanque was a regular reader of an occasional contributor to Books and Company.

Our writers

Ronald Blythe

There must be few regions without their local authors and few local authors who do not in time become affectionately accepted as authentic voices of a particular area. A remarkable number of writers struggled away in cottages and farmhouses during my East Anglian youth, rare birds for the most part, so that when my mother pointed to a tweedy person in Stour Street and said, 'That is Adrian Bell, the author,' I stared hard. His celebrity at that moment rose from his having written a rural trilogy a few miles down river, which was being much praised, *Corduroy, Silver Ley* and *The Cherry Tree,* gentle autobiographical novels about a young man farming a few acres of the deplorable agricultural scene which was Suffolk between the wars. Many years later, when I myself had joined the 'local authors', he and I met now and then in bookshops and liked each other. His father was the journalist Robert Bell and his son Martin would become the brilliant war-reporter for the BBC. Adrian had collaborated on a book entitled *Men and the Fields* with my old friend John Nash, these fields being the land which stretched behind my present home, Bottengoms Farm, and Adrian's Creems Farm. We could look into the gardens of these ancient Stour Valley houses from each other's fences. When I first glimpsed him Adrian's wealth, unknown to me at that moment, was three guineas for each *Times* crossword puzzle that he set – over four and a half thousand eventually – the first being on February 1 1930. So as well as riding his bicycle along our lanes to note shepherds and ploughmen, he was deep in 23 across and 4 down. Not long after his death in 1980 – he and his wife Marjory had by then long ago left the Stour for the Waveney – I was re-reading the famous trilogy which was now curiously interwoven with all our Suffolk lives and I noted how our children mystified him, that 'ragged and chubby throng with angel eyes but acquisitive hands that made a procession of Benfield Street morning and evening,' and who were found in the fields without shoes or stockings on winter days eating mangolds, some of whose fathers were drunks and some of whose homes were unfit for human habitation, and some who, for all the hardships, shone from some undiscoverable source of good living. And he was mystified by their mothers too, 'thin and pale as so many country wives are.' All around him the new cry on the farms was 'Buy a tractor and sack some men.' Towards the end of *Silver Ley* he gives a wonderful portrait of his neighbours, then almost the last of the 'old people,' as they are known. They had come to his house to ring hand-bells on Boxing Day 1928.

'The old narrow bricks used to ring with their steel-shod feet and their voices to vibrate with an unfamiliar depth and huskiness here within walls. Somehow, seen suddenly away from their usual background of acres and sky, the texture of their lives stood out the more. The brows that one never saw now, when their caps were off, the wiry, rebellious hair, like patches of standing corn that the wind had whirled awry, their clean rough shirts and collars, blue and red striped, the heavy festooned watch-chain, the thick waistcoat without points, the leather-bound cuff, the rosy cheek, the swart hand – the roughness and cleanness and well-mendedness of their clothes, the colour of them and the slow stir that even the smallest movements seemed to make about them. Their cheeks had been painted by the air and light. They were touched always and all days by limitlessness – by great views, winds. And they brought the stare of it in with them somehow. It was like the light of the snow in the room.'

Adrian Bell, our more than sufficient apologist, our 'one of us' had been born in Manchester and brought up in Chelsea. Like three other authors we liked to claim as our own, W.H. Freeman, C. Henry Warren and A.E Coppard, he was a Victorian – just. I met each of them briefly before I too began to write. Being so deeply and helplessly indigent, I had to be absorbed not claimed. Thinking suddenly of Adrian, the lights of his old home winking across the river at me every night and his fields now being rumbled over by the contract ploughman's multi-bladed monster, I began to think of why we loved Freeman, Warren and Coppard so and whether we still did. Could they still deserve their once-magic place in our localised hearts? Their small books clung together on the shelf, A.E. Coppard's the elegant Cape Travellers' Library edition, C. Henry Warren on wartime paper, W.H. Freeman in handy Chatto and Windus format. What an age since they were opened. Conscience strikes me the blow it saves for neglect.

Something phenomenal then occurs. It means that, after a generation or so, it is not we who have to put our local authors in the correct literary order, their works do it for themselves. Books know their place.

Thus, little volumes entitled *Adam and Eve and Pinch Me,*

Fishmonger's Fiddle, and *The Black Dog* took bright precedent, and with ease, of every other book drawn from these parts. Such marvellous short stories still! Why are we not all reading them? Not that A.E. Coppard came from round here or drew on us to any recognizable extent for his stories. Unlike our other authors, he could be said to have come from nowhere, as genius often did in 1878, the year he was born at Folkestone. He went to school until he was nine and then he was set to tailoring. But when he was thirty he became a clerk in Oxford, took what he required from extra-mural studies, and began to write – like Chekhov they said. Like a native writer of genius for various native places, including Suffolk and Essex. I was in my twenties and he in his seventies when we met, a slight young-old man with a wren's eye for the minutiae which can make up the whole.

Of course, Coppard's were only residential qualifications where we East Anglians were concerned. He had to write somewhere so he wrote between the wars in Southwold, where he might have patronised the teashop owned by George Orwell's sister, there being few better spots for observing the English at that time, and at Duton Hill, Dunmow, during the fifties. But if either of these addresses meant that those who had some permanent right to them could discover themselves nobly or scandalously obvious in his tales, they would have been disappointed. They were there all right but too penetrated, too found out to be tolerable. Let an author do what he can for local characters, even if he does his worst with them, but let him know everything about Us. Often the Coppard short story is quite lengthy. It can only end when it must. Reading him, you feel that no editor is standing over him saying 'two to four thousand words.' They start circumstantially. 'On a fine afternoon in April, a man is sitting at the foot of an ash tree beside the pool of water on Peck Common.' Although some of them cross into aristocratic or bourgeois territory with daring ease, most are concerned with the post-Dickensian race of country people who survived until almost the breakneck speed of late-twentieth century development of everything. The language they speak has been listened to and faultlessly written down. When critics mentioned him in the same breath as de Maupassant or Turgenev, he told them that his masters were those who sang old English ballads in the pubs or who told tall old English tales. The point was that A.E. Coppard could *write* – write good rural authors under the table. He is the master of lust in the front room and also of the delicacy of certain situations where the wrong word would make the roof cave in. I re-read him with wonderment and realised that V.S. Pritchett must have learned something from him, not to mention the young H.E. Bates. Coppard's job at Oxford was confidential clerk to an engineering works and his stories could be called a lyric confiding of the private life of English country people. It was a life which lay hidden from commonplace observation, dense as this was with class, trade and oddity, but never from him. His art gave him the entré to it. 'You want a farmer for farming that's true Mrs Sadgrove, but when it comes to marriage, we...' The rule book lies open at every applicable page in a Coppard story but between the lines men and women of all ages are having a high old time.

Some local novels are so much in the air that we believe and say that we have read them without our so much as opening them. This osmotic familiarity related to W.H. Freeman's *Joseph and his Brethren* where I was concerned. I even remember recommending it to those who came to my classes on East Anglian writers, and praising it knowledgeably. This story, set around 1920s Saxmundham, was as I knew in some detail, about a labourer who had become a farmer and who worked his family to death, being 'allus on the goo,' as they still say in those parts. You must read *Joseph and his Brethren,* I said, and in my own mind it was firmly positioned as a classic.

One day, Hugh Barrett author of that most realistic account of a farm apprenticeship, *Early One Morning,* and I went off to Ipswich to see the Suffolk Show, and who should be in the beer-tent but W.H. Freeman, a legendary figure whom I had thought long dead. He was tall, amused, ancient, handsome, dealing deftly with my wonder. The inevitable question had to come – why had he stopped writing? For as well as Joseph he had published half a dozen country novels, all well-received, as they say. 'We took up ballroom-dancing instead, my wife and I.' Before the Suffolk novels he had wandered, Laurie-Lee like, in France, Spain and Italy. The hard graft of Europe's peasantry had not been so distant from that of the Saxmundham experience during the farming depression, he had noted. Discovering Joseph on the Suffolk Books stall, I purchased it for £1.25 and he wrote his famous name in it. A little later his housekeeper telephoned to tell me of his death and what should she do with all his papers? There were so many of them. 'Take them to the Suffolk Records Office, please,' and this she did.

That evening I read *Joseph and his Brethren* and saw that having our actual villages in a tale sanctified them in our eyes. Somebody at the time called it 'a slow, rich, solid book' and I could see that it had a built-in endurance. It deals openly with farm monotony, farm illnesses, farm greed, farm cussedness and primly with farm sex. All the writer's art has gone into getting the dialect and the work right and both are true achievements. The miracle or the mystery remains. How did young Harold Freeman, Classical Scholar of Christ Church Oxford, hippy traveller of the warm south, occasional schoolmaster and mere Suffolk-watcher, get us so right? How flattered we are when someone sings our grimness, the hard rows which fate deals us and our glorious stinginess. As the combine trundles across the millennial harvest in a cloud of dust, shall we not take *Joseph and his Brethren* and murmur, 'Ah, those were the days!'

I spent a few hours with C Henry Warren shortly before I, too, became a freelance writer. I was staying at Little Easton Rectory and he had come over from Finchingfield for lunch, which at the Rectory began at tea-time, the Rector not rising till midday. He was enormous, some twenty stone, and a fine pianist, the huge hands drawing Scarlatti, a favourite, from the Steinway with a powerful delicacy, the huge feet under the cassock touching the pedals so persuasively that the music hung in the air like sound-embroidery. The room was chilly and the dining room plain cold. The Rector opened its window, and gave us cocktails. Both C. Henry Warren and I were thin and shivered. Soup would warm us up, promised the Rector. Most of what we talked about has gone. Warren was celebrated in this lovely bit of Essex for a wartime book, *England is a Village*, and he remains one of the best describers of 'War Age' Britain, with the Spitfires hurtling over ploughed-up pastures and the English countryside under threat of invasion as it had never been loved before. He was an early BBC man and had been an assistant editor of the *Radio Times*, when its pages contained exquisite line-drawings by Eric Frasier and other artists. Artists were everywhere in this corner of Essex. Warren's illustrator had been Thomas Hennell, killed during the war, and whilst I experienced a nervous exultation at the thought of going off to write, in the 1950s, Warren, it seemed to me, continued to wear the climate of the early Forties like an inescapable miasma. 'I wish you well,' he said. Looking again at his *The Land is Yours* a resurgence of the special melancholy of the country writer in his cottage wells up from the speckled paper. What the farmers did in 1943 around Finchingfield is indeed correctly stated with great formality of purpose and all Warren's writing of this period is high on exactitude and a gift for the rural historian. But when it was first published people read it as an inventory of an inheritance which they could well soon lose. So time alters response. As lunch dragged on into early evening and the Rector returned to the piano, trying to get Warren to stay the night, I could see him struggling to find an irrefutable excuse for his leaving. At last he did so.

'The Rayburn will go out.'

Ronald Blythe is a novelist, essayist and critic. His books include The Age of Illusion, Akenfield, The Assassin, Going to Meet George *and* Outsiders. *He was born in Suffolk and lives in the Stour Valley. He has received the Heinemann Award and the Benson Medal for Literature. His latest book is* Aftermath: Collected Essays.

The ghost stories of M.R. James

John Francis

Montague Rhodes James died in 1936 at Eton just as they were singing Nunc Dimittis in Chapel. I found this comfortable fact in M.R. James. *An Informal Portrait* by Michael Cox. So the passing of the man who had filled and is still filling the minds of his readers with such exquisite apprehension, such sweet perturbation, seems to have been almost enviable. You feel that the Angel of Death showed a proper sense of decorum.

As I read the *Informal Portrait* I was struck by how fortunate James had been. His life was a smooth progression from distinguished pillar to eminent post. Unlike so many of his contemporaries he seems never to have been blown upon by gusts of religious doubt. I recollect that he had beautiful manners and reservoirs of tact – he was much in demand as a provider of memorial texts- yet he was not complacent. A complacent man could not have written in *A Neighbour's Landmark.*

> The sun was down behind the hill and the light was off the fields, and when the clock bell in the church tower struck seven I thought no longer of kind mellow evenings of rest and scents of flowers and woods on the evening air, and of how someone on a farm a mile or two off would be saying, ' How clear Betton bell sounds tonight,

after the rain!'; but instead, images came to me of dusty beams and creeping spiders and savage owls up in the tower and forgotten graves and their ugly contents below and of flying Time and all that it had taken from my life.

Less than a decade after his death, probably in the summer of 1941, a semi-circle of small boys sat on the lawn of a garden in Salisbury Cathedral Close listening to a Mr Arnold reading aloud *The Five Jars* by M.R. James.

The Close was, I found out later, appropriate to one's first encounter with MRJ for in his Preface to his *Collected Ghost Stories* he wrote that 'the Cathedrals of Barchester and Southminster were blends of Canterbury, Salisbury and Hereford.'

Mr Arnold didn't have time to finish reading *The Five Jars* so we were left dangling, in my case until 1956, when I acquired a second-hand copy. I have it still and often re-read it. I wonder why it is not more widely known.

On the run from games and the maths master I was gratified to find myself in the sickroom at boarding school, comfortably unwell with a cold that had turned 'chesty.' My sense of well-being was augmented by the uncouth cries coming from the playing fields and the sight of the rain dashing against the window. The sick room had a shelf heavy with books by Arthur Mee but among the Mee was a book, *The Ghost Stories of an Antiquary* by M.R. James. That name! Perhaps after all this time I might discover how things turned out. Of course it did not contain *The Five Jars*. But even so, I started on the first story, *Canon Alberic's Scrapbook.*

'It was time to ring the Angelus. A few pulls at the reluctant rope and the great bell Bertrande, high in the tower, began to speak and swung her voice up among the pines

> and down to the valleys, loud with mountain streams, calling the dwellers on those lonely hills to remember and repeat the salutation to her whom he called Blessed among women.

I was thrilled and terrified by the whole story but there was something about that passage that stirred and excited me almost to the point of pain. I was the bell. I was, for a giddy moment, the pines, before mutating into a mountain stream. Nothing I had read before had had this effect. I had sucked the sugar out of plots, yes, but I had never known that prose could be music. King George had stood up when he heard the Hallelujah Chorus for the first time, an unwary monarch surprised by beauty. Perhaps I lay to attention in bed.

Was I stirred partly because Bertrande and all her sisters were silent in their sleep during the war-time restrictions?

The stories start quite slowly – indeed, one is soothed by period details. What exactly are 'the Piccadilly weepers' that, together with the thin face are singled out for mention at the start of *The Tractate Middoth*? No doubt a style of moustache long out of fashion. He of 'the weepers' is entering a library and libraries are useful places, cosy almost. Think again. All the main characters in James's stories are well-heeled gentlemen who come before us flanked by servants and usually devoted ones at that. It is this aspect of their lives, their freedom from domestic work, that makes these men free to visit libraries, to saunter learnedly through remote parts of France in order to photograph cathedrals, that makes them distinctly enviable. It puts me in mind of Sherlock Holmes, who had to deal with many villains but never had to make his own bed or toast. The reader who does have to make his own bed and toast would be hard put to dash off at a moment's notice, as the Rector of Parsbury does in *The Treasure of Abbot Thomas,* to The Continent. The hansom may be slower than the minicab but as his means of getting to Paddington, Sherlock Holmes would find it entirely reliable. Our lives are perhaps meaner and drabber but society is more equitably organised and no one may expect to enjoy himself overmuch, so no wonder we enjoy shuffling off, via books, to an unfairer, more privileged age and 'a stately dame of some fifty summers' who desires to make a rose garden.

In the ghost stories, James often had characters who warn against change, especially if the one proposed seems to insult some tradition or whispered warning. In order to make space for the rose garden, an old post, a tentative sybil, says enough to deter a more imaginative garden. Something extremely nasty is seen and Mrs Anstruther has to go abroad to recuperate.

What sort of man was M.R. James? Michael Cox has gone into things thoroughly and gives him a good report, regrets that he did not know him personally. There is another good sign, at least for some – he enjoyed P.G. Wodehouse.

After the First World War, when the pall of dust was gradually settling, the survivors could make out some few structures which, much damaged, they thought worthy of preserving and repairing. Others – Lytton Strachey being of their number – were inclined to insert their sticks of dynamite and after the detonation start again from scratch.

There is a passage in *An Episode of Cathedral History* which pre-echoes the jolly vandalism of that period.

> It was in 1840 that the wave of the Gothic revival smote the Cathedral of Southminster. 'There was a lot of lovely stuff went then, sir,' said Worby with a sigh.' My father couldn't

> hardly believe it when he got orders to clear out the choir. There was a new Dean just come in and my father had been apprenticed to a good firm of joiners in the city and knew what good work was when he saw it. Crool it was, he used to say, all that beautiful wainscot oak, as good as the day it was put up, and garlands of foliage and fruit and lovely gilding work on the coats of arms and the organ pipes.'

Many of the stories carry warnings against curiosity and the idea that because some act is feasible it automatically becomes desirable. That which is not consistent with the new Dean's notion of the Gothic must be cleared out, destroyed. Old Dr Ayloff insists that moving the pulpit is a mistake.

> 'But what sense could there be, my dear Doctor, in leaving it where it is when we're fitting up the rest of the choir in a totally different style? What reason could be given?'
>
> 'Reason! Reason!,' said Dr Ayloff, ' If you, young man, would only listen to reason a little and not always be asking for it we should get on better. But there, I've said my say.'

After that it is possible to feel some sympathy for the Dean, who is operating on a rational level, while Dr Ayloff is working on instinct and intuition.

But when the pulpit is gone and an altar tomb is revealed, quite plain but with a gap between the slabs which make up one of its sides, it is the doctor who is proved to be justified. Along with the pulpit goes Dr Ayloff, taken 'painfully at night.' And then 'the nuisance that is still remembered as 'the crying' set in.' Opinion turns against the Dean and he is obliged to agree that the altar-tomb should be re-sealed. While this is being attempted, something erupts from the tomb and knocks the dean over. 'A thing like a man, all over hair and two great eyes to it.' Dean Burscough happens to be looking the other way and so literally never knew what hit him.

For James there was always something behind every arras and best not to go poking about. He walked about on pie-crust, we all do, although many people suppose it to be solid earth. Caution and respect are cardinal virtues. Take Baxter, who so far forgot himself as to boil up the bones of the dead in order to purloin their eyesight, in *A View from a Hill*. The owners of the bones, forming a ghostly escort, come to take him away. A chance onlooker, observing this kidnapping from an upper window, is advised 'Tis best to mind your own business. Put in your head.'

On the first page of *A Neighbour's Landmark*, James himself comes into sharp focus.

> 'Remember if you please,' said my friend, looking at me over his spectacles, 'that I am a Victorian by birth and education and that the Victorian tree may not unreasonably be expected to bear Victorian fruit. Further, remember that an immense quantity of clever and thoughtful rubbish is now being written about the Victorian age.'

Surely that passage is by way of being an outline sketch for a self-portrait and the view expressed about 'clever and thoughtful rubbish' the Jamesian opinion of Lytton Strachey.

When Lady Wardrop, an expert on mazes, at last gains entry

to the maze inherited by Mr Humphrey's example, she is glad to have seen it of course, but she is anxious not to linger.

> 'I shouldn't like to take liberties here. I have the feeling that it might be resented. Now confess,' she went on, turning and facing Humphreys, ' don't you feel, haven't you felt ever since we came in here, that a watch is being kept on us and that if we overstepped the mark in any way there would be a – well, a pounce?'

Lady Wardrop's misgivings serve as armour or protective clothing. Mr Humphreys, less alert to nuance, is taught, like Mrs Anstruther in *The Rose Garden*, a sharp lesson.

In *Stories I have Tried to Write*, a rueful and light-hearted essay, James concludes, 'Late on Monday night, a toad came into my study and, though nothing so far has seemed to link itself with this appearance, I feel that it may not be quite prudent to brood over topics which open the interior eye to the presence of more formidable visitants. Enough said.'

The tone is light, humorous. People often joke about their anxieties. Laughter can strike like lightening at funerals. *Nervous laughter.* Why, the words were made for one another.

M.R. James was shown into a first-class compartment by the circumstances of his birth. The journey of his life was accomplished, to outward view at least, smoothly and with no incidents on the line and he reached the terminus just as they were singing the Nunc Dimittis in chapel. And yet throughout that long and seemingly comfortable journey, I feel that he saw with his interior eye an invisible companion and heard a voice which no one else could hear make an unsettling observation, point out some unwelcome token, a toad, perhaps, crouched on his Gladstone bag, that was watching him.

Maybe we all have such invisible companions but only a select few are aware of these spectral attendants.

Enough said.

John Francis was a regular reader of and occasional contributor to Books and Company.

An inheritance

Philip Hensher

My grandmother had two sets of books. One was bright red, a set of H.G. Wells's novels. Whoever issued those was an anti-commercial genius of the very highest order, since the set omits all the science fiction and speculative work – no *Time Machine,* no *War of the Worlds,* no *Island of Doctor Moreau.* Instead, there were *The World of William Clissold, Ann Veronica* and *The New Machiavelli.* As a child, I was drawn to the magical and mysterious title *Tono-Bungay.* I am sorry to say that rumbustious work with its ravishing epilogue, "Night and the Open Sea" still closely resembles my idea of what a really good novel ought to be.

All the same, the lack of alien invaders and freakish underworld monsters cast a pall over one half of my grandmother's library. The other half is so familiar to me that I had to concentrate to think what colour the binding is. It is a sort of purply-brown, imitation morocco. Really, it is Dickens-coloured, because these were the books my grandmother loved, and the way I first got to love Dickens.

My grandmother was not an educated person but she loved and respected education, as that generation so often did. She made sure her son took up a musical instrument, learning to play Haydn, Beethoven and Chopin in the front room of her terraced house in St Helier. It is an enormous

London County Council public housing estate, built in the late 1920s and early 1930s to re-home families from often desperate housing in inner London. Before that, the family had lived in roughly the same square mile of Bethnal Green, and were clay pipe makers before that peculiar trade collapsed some time in the mid 19th century.

Later generations- and possibly some people at the time-saw education as a passport to social improvement. I don't know that my grandmother did. I think she liked it for itself. She was forever recommending novels to her bookworm grandson, in old age. She didn't acquire the sets of Dickens and Wells because she thought it would be good for her son. She clearly read them herself with some enjoyment and when they came down to me after her death in 1976, it was obvious that she had read some more than once and others not at all. Like many people, she could not get on with the angry later novels that critics have so admired in the last fifty years. When I opened up *Our Mutual Friend* in the late 1970s, the glue in the binding went off like a pistol shot, not inappropriately. On the other hand, *David Copperfield* flowed like butter, much loved, its pages much turned over.

As the small explosion of *Our Mutual Friend*'s binding suggests, these are terrible books as objects. The steel typeface is very hard on the eyes, heavy and rather nineteenth-century in style. The illustrations show some signs of wear, and for me, "Phiz" has never cast much of an enchantment, with his unvarying puddingy faces and his lack of a way with heroines. The paper must be simply saturated with acid, judging by the way it has yellowed and grown friable in less than a century. I dare say the texts aren't up to much, either.

Still, I love them because that was what Dickens first

looked like to me and the way in which Dickens comes to you will always be in the garb of a lover. I've tried, without much success, to discover what they are and where they come from. They bear no date, and the publisher is recorded as Hazell, Watson and Viney – it was not really a publisher, I believe, but an Aylesbury jobbing printer, large and successful enough to merit its own war memorial when dozens of its workers were killed in the Great War. I've come to the conclusion that my grandmother came by a set of Dickens through a newspaper offer, some time in the early 1930s. I suspect it was an offer by Beaverbrook's *Daily Express*. Perhaps Hazell, Watson and Viney printed sets of Dickens as a speculative venture into publishing and a newspaper offer was an attempt to offload stock. It seems the most likely way for my grandmother and for thousands of other readers, to acquire a set like this. (You can still, very easily, find the Hazell Watson and Viney set for sale in second-hand bookshops and online – it will never be worth a lot).

They came to my grandmother for not very much, and they came to me for absolutely nothing. But one day you open a volume up, and the riches seem incalculable. I was an awful little literary snob and the first one I read was *Bleak House*. I'm not totally sure I followed the detail of the plot, and I have a definite memory of feeling frustrated, as Dickens passes you among minor characters, from the Smallweeds to the Military Bassoonist to the Shooting Gallery with no very obvious aim in mind. But really, he had me at Mrs Jellyby, and had me all over again at Caddy Jellyby's fiancé, Prince Turveydrop.

What is it about Dickens? Why did I finish with *Bleak House*, and go straight on to *Little Dorrit*? (I said I was an awful little literary snob – it took me years to admit how supreme

David Copperfield is, from beginning to end). From David Kynaston's wonderful social history of post-war England, we learn that at the end of the Second World War Dickens was still one of the five most popular authors borrowed from public libraries. From Jonathan Rose's magisterial and vitally important history of working class endeavour, *The Intellectual Life of the English Working Classes* I discovered that my grandmother's interests and enthusiasm were not at all remarkable; were probably towards the lower end of the self-improvement scale, in fact. She would never have joined a political group, or gone to a public lecture, or carried out a course of reading. I think, actually, she only loved Dickens. These historians give us important and exciting facts; what they can't altogether give us is that intensely living culture which went from Dickens, to a printer who believed they could make some money, to a newspaper which saw an opportunity, to my grandmother, and then to me. I've sometimes bought more reputable, reliable and readable editions of Dickens for serious purposes since. On the other hand, when I think of Dickens, I think of that line of haematite-coloured spines.

The other day, an American writer said to me that he thought *Madame Bovary* had never been surpassed for realist fantasy. I must have hesitated, not really being much of a one of score-cards, and quickly he said to the company "You'll never get an English novelist to admit anyone's better than Dickens." He got his laugh; but on the other hand, I thought he was probably right.

Phillip Hensher is a columnist for The Independent, *Chief Book Reviewer for* The Spectator, *and a Granta Best of Young British novelist. He has written five novels,* Other Lulus, Kitchen Venom

(Winner of the Somerset Maugham Award), Pleasured, *the Booker-longlisted* The Mulberry Empire *and* The Fit, *and the Booker-shortlisted* The Northern Clemency, *and a collection of short stories,* The Bedroom of the Mister's House.

The man on the number 46 bus

Nick Harkaway

"Long afterwards," I read, giving my voice a bit of ominous depth, "the news came that all the donkeys were dead."

My fellow passengers on the 46 bus nodded. Yes, indeed. Marlowe's journey was never going to end well, and this was all the confirmation they needed. The woman with the potatoes said that the fellow probably shouldn't have gone, and the two schoolkids cheered, dead donkeys being a delight to all mankind.

Blame Joseph Conrad. I hadn't intended to inflict on my fellow travellers an impromptu public performance of *Heart of Darkness,* it just happened that way. I love Conrad's book but for some reason I can't get into it unless I read it aloud. Since sitting in the back of the bus muttering into my lap would have put me in the loony category, I'd let my voice get just a shade louder so that anyone within a couple of rows could hear that I was reading the book in my hand and generally behaving in a coherent if eccentric way and there was no need to have me arrested.

People in North London, of course, are used to others randomly doing art at them and by and large they don't object unless you're part of something like the 'get Britain singing' campaign. A man in a baseball cap actually moved a row nearer so he could hear. The woman with the potatoes took her headphones out for a listen. The schoolkids live-texted the whole thing to someone else, who apparently didn't like Conrad and thought Maya Angelou would have been better.

The interesting thing about this – aside from the spectacle of a thirty-something author making a twit of himself on public transport, which is always good for a giggle – is that it highlights something about Conrad's writing: he lends himself to speech. I find the same with P.G. Wodehouse and Sir Arthur Conan Doyle – although it's not so pronounced. I can happily read either of them in the quiet of my head. On the other hand, I'd rather read them out loud. The choice of words is fluid and some bits beg for spoken emphasis. You can find voices and ways of speaking hidden in the text. Wodehouse's prolonged shaggy dog stories usually culminate in a Shakespearian sort of reveal in which it turns out that the chap pretending to be a doctor is the jilted lover of the bird engaged to the fellow who actually is a doctor but is posing as a novelist because he's secretly in love with the fiancée of the first bloke, and the whole bunch of them are in trouble because someone's uncle has pinched a priceless tiara to punish the vicar for being rude about a box of scones, but it's okay because the terrifying aunt whose wrath will descend upon them all and result in poverty and disgrace has just been caught for valid and honourable reasons dressed as a postman and peering over the hedge at a local racehorse being trained in secret by the brother of the unwanted fiancée of the first bloke who isn't really a doctor.

And Wodehouse, being Wodehouse, makes all that perfectly simple and reasonable and utterly hilarious, but it's even funnier if you can read the "I don't follow you" and "Good

Lord, Caruthers, are you wearing a turkey?" and so on in appropriate tones of alarm and delight.

Perhaps not all of that is Wodehouse's doing. There's a sense of conspiracy in live reading, a collusion between the reader and the audience which makes for great comedy. It plays with tragedy too, of course, but to my mind not so strongly. The urge to get away from crisis and trauma separates you from someone who's reading about horrible things – which is a tribute to Conrad, who can hang on to you in spite of it.

Conan Doyle is different again – in part because he has a spread of characters to whom one responds in different ways. Sherlock Holmes is a snappish, brilliant, arrogant man. He's hard to sympathise with but one wants to believe that one could do better than Watson at following his wild leaps of inference and logic. Deduction, like comedy, brings us inside the circle, which is maybe why the Holmes stories are so frequently adapted and performed.

It's not Holmes, though, who really makes me want to read aloud from the Conan Doyle stable. It is his diametric opposite, the somewhat neglected and wonderful Etienne Gerard.

Brigadier Gerard, whose stories are told by the great man himself without the faintest blush at extolling his own bravery and brilliance, is as far from Holmes as you can go without falling off the edge of the character map. He loves widely, unwisely, prodigiously. He admires women and duels men. He gives his word in an instant but holds to it for ever, is rarely introspective, and thinks entirely with his heart. He lives in a perpetual, puppyish now, and is constantly up to his neck in disaster. He serves in the army of Napoleon, whom he worships, but who occasionally is moved by great emotion to remark that Gerard is as thick as a board. Etienne Gerard is an actual Anti-Holmes. And yet, honestly would you rather be in the company of an ascetic, irritable genius with a spidery, chess player's mind, or at an inn in the French countryside with a loud, generous nitwit who will drop everything and devote his life to solving your problems, and whose success rate is every bit as high as his opposite's?

One thing's for sure: the joy of reading Gerard to a group is endless. It takes them a few seconds to realize that this pompous popinjay is also a hero worthy of the name and that everything will come out right in the end, and then they're sold. Doyle's faux-French heroic prose rolls off the tongue and Gerard's own frequent monologues on bravery, women and horses on the one hand reveal him for the dimwit he is and on the other, give glimpses of a genuine, empathic soul amid the bluster. Here is a character drawn in the mirror of his own inflated ego and all the more sympathetic for it – especially as it's just possible he's as much of a hero as he believes. In the end, after all, Napoleon does wish for more like Gerard.

There's a counter-group, too – writers I love, but cannot read except in silence. Neal Stephenson is one. The author of *Snow Crash* and the *Baroque Cycle* writes discursive, parenthetical prose for a textual age. His presentation of seventeenth century England in *Quicksilver* is a match for Doyle's own Micah Clarke. Both of them show a country in the throes of deep strife, debate, and social change as it seeks to answer questions about the place of the individual in society and the nature of man and God, while at the same time Hooke and Newton are disputing whether light is a wave or a particle and the scientific age is arriving at speed. With *Quicksil-*

ver, though, I want to lock myself in a room and suck up the information through my eyes, rather than share the story with my voice. That's not to say Stephenson can't write to be read aloud – he absolutely can and does. It just isn't a constant with him. Similarly, I could read Jeanette Winterson's *The Passion* aloud, but it feels wrong: the story is so intensely, gorgeously intimate, I'd feel as if I was gossiping.

I wonder – I have no idea – whether these writers read aloud to themselves or their families and friends as part of the creative process. I find myself, from time to time, reading the words as I type them, or reading back what I've scrawled by hand. I read the printed drafts of my own work to an empty room or very occasionally to my wife. The patterns of spoken speech are woven in from the start. Wodehouse, according to story, had a corkboard divided into five sections, A-E, and put bad pages at the bottom and great pages at the top, moving them up through the editing process and considering the book unfinished if there were any pages left in the lower rows. What the rumour doesn't say is if one of the hurdles – possibly the last – was whether a passage could be or even demanded to be read aloud.

The 46 bus isn't the perfect venue for all this, of course. It jolts about and I get a bit carsick. I'm amazed that so many people were delighted by the madman on the back seat with his *Heart of Darkness*, but it isn't an experiment I propose to revisit too often. Not everyone would be grateful for Gerard or Cuthbert Banks or even for slices of Josh Bazell's hard-boiled *Beat The Reaper* (there's a book which could get me arrested for sure.)

All the same, it's a tribute to the power of language – and to Conrad in particular – that he pushed me to do it in the first place, and then ensorcelled my contemporaries on the journey to King's Cross. In an age of distraction, the spoken word retains a power of its own.

Nick Harkaway is the author of The Gone-Away World. *He was born in 1972, and lives in London with his wife, Clare. He reads fanatically, eclectically, and not always wisely, which is probably the most rewarding way to do it.*

Coming in from the outside

Inga-Stina Ewbank

Books are company and if you grow up in a minority language, much of that company is foreign and yet, because translated, it is speaking to you in your own tongue. As I was growing up in Sweden it never occurred to me that my English contemporaries did not read novels with footnotes saying that six English miles equal ten kilometres or explaining untranslatable puns. These things became part of the fiction, made its world of places and people with unpronounceable names (try saying 'the Marshalsea' or 'Veneering' or 'Jarndyce' giving each vowel and consonant its full phonetic value) all the more exciting and exotic. I did not have the kind of multi-lingual childhood that George Steiner describes in *After Babel.* German, English and French, in that order, were school subjects not ways into literature. My father had taught himself to read -but not to speak -English, and there were plenty of Tauchnitz volumes on our shelves but their cheap yellowing paper and disintegrating covers did not invite forays into English as she is written.

And then, at the age of eighteen and on a scholarship to a wonderful Liberal Arts College in the United States, I was propelled headlong into English literature and discovered that this and not mathematics, as I had planned, was what I wanted to spend the rest of my life in and on. In that first term, there was Shakespeare, which had until then meant memorising, in the final year of the Gymnasium, 'To be or not to be' and 'The quality of mercy,' and which now meant the English language so used as to work miracles of creation. And, bliss, it meant Katherine Hepburn (never mind her age) being Rosalind in *As You Like It,* in Minneapolis. And there were the metaphysical poets, unheard of at school, where literature meant European literary history and the chief English landmarks were Gray's *The Bard* and Young's *Conjectures on Original Composition* – because, we were told, they started the pre-Romantic Movement. And there were Thackeray and George Eliot and *The Way of All Flesh,* when all I had known of the Victorian novel was (translated) Dickens.

But of course, in the midst of this dawn there were drawbacks to having grown up in the wrong company. One of those moments etched into memory with a permanent power to make me squirm was when a professor, visiting from England and who liked my essay on *The Duchess of Malfi,* asked what contemporary English literature I had read and I replied 'James Hilton and Nevil Shute.' I squirm when I remember the look in his eyes, as if at something the cat had brought in and the way it measured my fall in his estimation. Vulnerable then, I now, after forty years of teaching English students English literature, wish I could go back, and put up a defence for *Goodbye, Mr Chips* and *The Pied Piper,* as company of the 'right' kind. A defence, that is, of the importance of remembering that English literature looks different when seen from the outside and that the way into it is to acquire a love of reading at as early an age as possible. Appetite before discrimination.

Again I have to be autobiographical because I was fortunate

enough to grow up in a context where books were indeed the best company, in the remote Swedish countryside in a pre-television age, far from libraries but with parents who, while not literary in any professional sense, bought and read books and allowed uncensored access to whatever was on the shelves. It meant that I made little distinction between books written for children and those for adults. Angela Brazil's boarding school stories, Kipling's *Stalkey and Co,* Dickens' Dotheboys Hall and the public school in *Goodbye, Mr Chips,* all came together into one wondrous world, more phantasmagoric than English. *Little Women* seemed tame and colourless compared to *Little Dorrit,* which I read and re-read, wishing that I too had a father in prison to do noble things for. When, a little later England, began to take shape as a 'real' country it was in terms of extremes. At one end there was the gouty aristocratic grandfather of Little Lord Fauntleroy, at the other, the starving paupers of Jack London's *People of the Abyss,* all so different from the solid welfare ways of democratic Sweden. And, as I read my way through Kipling there grew a sense not so much of the British Empire as of an enviably mysterious world elsewhere. As an insider now, I know that I should be as wary of Kipling's colonialism as of Mr Chips's patriarchalism or the Pied Piper's chauvinism. But undeniably, these books were better company when, seen from the outside, they were not 'isms but stories.

Good stories translate more readily than verbal subtleties – which is, of course why translating poetry is such a near-impossible challenge, and, more specifically, why there was little English poetry apart from Byron on our shelves.

But there was Nevil Shute's novel *The Pied Piper,* which has its own story. That of the book of an elderly Englishman trying, just after the Fall of France in 1940, to make his way back to England from a fishing holiday in the Jura mountains and finding himself responsible for the transit of one child after another, all of whom he manages to keep happy by cutting them whistles from hazel twigs and all of whom he eventually brings to a safe haven, having faced every mortal danger with understated British courage. Published in 1942, *The Pied Piper* must have been translated almost immediately into Swedish, the language of a neutral country which was feeling increasingly embarrassed, even guilty, about its neutrality. The book came into the house in the middle of the war and my mother was so moved by it that she felt she had to share the experience. There was in the parish a sewing circle of women, who met fortnightly to stitch away and drink ersatz coffee while the pastor read to them from some edifying book, to which they half-listened – rather as in the first act of Ibsen's *Pillars of Society*, except that these ladies did not sew moral underwear for fallen women but worked elaborate embroideries which they then, at an annual auction, sold and themselves bought back at exorbitant prices, the money going to good causes. The Pastor somewhat grudgingly allowed my mother to persuade him to replace the currently uplifting volume with *The Pied Piper*. He read it aloud, bowdlerising the odd oath and reference to sex as he went along and for weeks the circle was transfixed. For a group of farmers' wives in middle Sweden, who would never normally touch a work of fiction, this book did more than Churchill could to justify the ways of England in World War II.

I have written about my own experiences because in retrospect they seem to have been a microcosmic pointer to a general truth – that for good or ill, translation and transmission into another culture wipes out some of the distinction between high and middlebrow literature, which seems so clear when seen from within the original culture. No doubt this truth, if it is one, also has something to do with the sometimes seemingly bizarre choices of the Swedish academy when awarding the Nobel Prize for literature. How come, I have been asked, that it has been given to so many writers we haven't heard of?

This second question, if we take that 'we' as the average, educated English reader, touches on another aspect of coming into literature from the outside. There is a self-sufficiency about the English literary heritage which is justified by its richness and which nations less rich in this respect cannot afford but which can also take the form of insularity. Obviously I am again biased by my own early eclectic reading, where Zola was neither more nor less foreign than Dickens and Knut Hamsen more familiar than D.H. Lawrence. This is where the Nobel Prize comes in again, for the academy's verdicts had to some extent affected what was on my parents' shelves. So, for example, I came to develop a passion for the novels of Grazia Deledda who, wedged between Shaw and Bergson, had been the 1926 prize winner. I have never yet found anyone in England who has read her stark, clear novels of Sardinian life and landscape and who can share that passion – except a visiting Italian postgraduate student whom, paradoxically, I was supposed to guide through the syntactical convolutions and fine moral distinctions of the late Henry James.

Of course I am glad to be on the inside, to have caught up on essential English children's reading at the side of my own children and to have learned to treasure Henry James more than James Hilton and Wordsworth as much or more than

Byron. But the outsider is always there too, murmuring such questions as to whether it is right that English students should read the medieval play *Gammer Gurton's Needle* but not Goethe's *Faust*.

You can always tell an outsider from the way they read Kipling's poem *The English Flag* – 'What should they know of England/That only England know?'

Inga-Stina Ewbank knew only Swedish until the age of 19 but later studied and then taught English literature in America and the universties of Sheffield, Birmingham, Liverpool, London and Leeds, where she was a Professor. She translated several plays by Ibsen for the National Theatre. Inga-Stina Ewbank died in 2004.

www.longbarnbooks.com